Behold The Breath of Life

The 7 Most Extraordinary
Questions about Jesus Christ
Through the Eyes of Science

Copyright © 2018 by Dr. Dragos Bratasanu.
1st edition, January 2020

All rights reserved. No part of this book may be reproduced by any mechanical, photographical, or electronic process, on in the form of a phonographic recording, nor may it be stored in a retrieval system, transmitted, or otherwise be copied for public or private use - other than for "fair use" as brief quotations embodied in articles and reviews - without prior written permission from the publisher. The author of this book does not dispense medical advice or prescribe the use of any technique as a form of treatment for physical, emotional, or medical problems without the advice of a physician, either directly or indirectly. The intent of the author is only to offer information of a general nature to help you in your quest for wellbeing. In the event you use any of the information in this book for yourself, the author and the publisher assume no responsibility for your actions. For requests, write at corporate@drdragos.com or visit www.drdragos.com.

O, Father
Thy will be done.

TABLE OF CONTENTS

INTRODUCTION - Of Science and Truth   7

CHAPTER 1 - The Book of Life   23
Q1 - What is the Bible?

CHAPTER 2 - If You Can Only Believe   41
Q2 - Does Jesus heal the sick today?

CHAPTER 3 - One More Chance   69
Q3 - Does Jesus raise the dead today?

CHAPTER 4 - The Seed   79
Q4 - Does Jesus cast out demons today?

CHAPTER 5 - To Stand Before Him   105
Q5 - Where is Jesus Christ today?

CHAPTER 6 - Behold the Son   127
Q6 - Does Jesus appear to people today?

CHAPTER 7 - The Breath of Life   155
Q7 - Who is Jesus called the Christ?

EPILOGUE   169

REFERENCES   171

INTRODUCTION
Of Science and Truth

"In questions of science, the authority of a thousand is not worth the humble reasoning of a single individual" - Galileo Galilei

1.

Theo's office was covered with awards and diplomas from the aviation industry. On the wall behind his desk, books and files arranged in alphabetical order stacked from the ceiling to the floor, and aircraft models lined up for takeoff on each shelf.

"The documents you see here," said Theo and invited me to sit down, "contain lessons nobody wants to learn the hard way. Each air crash investigation hides the mystery of its own tragedy and reveals insights that have changed minds and hearts, even history itself. On the surface, these accidents seem to be about how technology fails and what we can do to improve it in the future, but once you dig deeper you discover that these tragic accounts have actually opened our eyes to understand ourselves better as human beings."

Theo moved his hand across the files stacked on the shelves and pulled one of them out.

"Let me tell you a story," he continued.

"A while ago, on September 7, 2011 I was on duty at the airport servicing a plane when a colleague walked inside the hangar and told us that an aircraft carrying the entire hokey team of Lokomotiv Yaroslavl had just crashed in Russia. Forty four passengers - the players, the coaching staff and the flight crew - all died on impact. The only survivor was Alexander Sizov, the flight engineer."

We soon learned that the airplane had ran off the end of the runway after a failed takeoff attempt and crashed into the Volga river less than a mile away from the airport. The local press released disturbing photos of the disaster immediately after. The ground was scorched and clouds of black smoke were rising from the wreckage. The tail of the airplane had become a heap of twisted metal still burning in the river. Two engines were smoldering somewhere far from the disintegrated remains of the fuselage. The landing gear was partially under water, and innumerable fragments of clothing, material, seats and hokey equipment were scattered as far as rescuers could see. Firefighters carried the dead bodies on stretchers, stacking them in bodybags on the banks of the river."

I flipped through the photographs released by the journalists as Theo continued speaking.

"Most of them were in their twenties, some in their early thirties" he said.

"Why did the plane crash?" I asked.

"The day was ideal for flying. Pilots followed normal takeoff procedures and before 4 o'clock in the afternoon the control tower gave them permission for takeoff. The crew was enthusiastic about this flight, it was an honor for them to carry the famous hokey team. The captain took control, thrusts engines to full power and accelerates down the runway. Everything runs perfectly."

The aircraft goes faster and faster. The flight engineer informs "Rotate!" which means the plane had reached the takeoff speed of 140 mph. The captain pulls the yoke to get the plane off the ground. Nothing happens. The airplane remains on the ground and continues to speed. The pilot pulls the yoke again, but the aircraft doesn't respond to his command. He tries again. Nothing. The crew has now about five seconds to abort the takeoff or to succeed, otherwise they will not be able to stop the aircraft before end of the runway. They have enough speed to fly but instead of lifting up, the aircraft keeps going faster and faster across the tarmac. The captain pulls the yoke again and again trying to get the plane airborne, but the aircraft doesn't respond to his commands. With each second, the situation was turning into a nightmare. The two pilots cannot get the plane off the ground and are heading high-speed towards the woods with a tank full of fuel. Passengers grip their seats as they realize something is terribly wrong. The aircraft speeds off the end of the runway and unto the grass field. The pilots shout in confusion and despair to get the plane off the ground. Suddenly the airplane takes off at a very steep angle, but it cannot fly in an almost vertical ascent. It climbs to about twenty feet altitude, hits a telecommunications tower with the left wing, then stalls and crashes into the river less than a mile away."

I flipped through the photographs released by the media as Theo shared the story. The entire Russian nation was mourning, newspapers showed.

"Investigators examined the incident step by step" Theo continued. "Weather was ideal for flying. The engines functioned properly. The aircraft was in good mechanical condition. The crew checked the airplane before takeoff and everything was working to standard. Technology was functioning in normal parameters. Tens of thousands of airplanes are taking off each day around the world, but this one didn't."

"What happened?" I asked.

"The only thing investigators had yet to verify was the crew's history and background. It turned out that both pilots were highly experienced. The two of them had more than 18,000 flight hours combined, which is more than two years spent in the cockpit in the air."

"The investigating committee released this report two months after the crash." Theo put on his glasses and started reading. "The immediate cause of the crash was the crew's erroneous actions, namely the pilot stepping on the brake pedals before raising the nose wheel because of the wrong position of his feet on the pedals during takeoff."

"What does this mean?" I said.

"One pilot was accelerating, while the other one was pressing the brakes."

"Why would they do that?"

"They didn't know they were doing it."

"I don't understand. What am I missing?"

"The truth..." Theo finally said and closed the file. "The very truth was missing."

"When investigators examined the crew's medical records they discovered evidence that the copilot had a neurological condition from which he had lost sensitivity in both legs. He was being treated in secret with drugs banned by the aviation industry and should't have been certified to fly. Because of his medical condition, he couldn't feel his feet and was pressing the brakes of the aircraft without even knowing. When you brake a plane, not only the wheels slow down, but the nose tilts downward and glues the aircraft to the ground. When you're speeding down the runway to take off, the nose must go upward, but pressing the brakes forces the plane to stick to the tarmac."

"When, with one last effort, they managed to get the plane off the ground, the aircraft snapped upwards at an angle too steep for it to fly. It stalled. At that point, as James Oberg, aviation expert and former NASA engineer noted in an interview for National Geographic, "you're a big hunk of metal and fuel and flesh just falling through the air." Investigators also discovered that the pilots had falsified documents stating they had completed training for this specific type of aircraft, which in fact they didn't."

I remained silent and my mind drifted to the innumerable times we entrust complete strangers with our lives.

"The public witnessed the tragedy, but the seed of this disaster was planted long time before" Theo continued. "One deceitful thought in the heart of man, once acted upon triggered a chain of events that unfolded over several years and ended in tragedy for 44 people, their families and friends."

"To conclude the story," Theo rested in his chair, "most of us understand how things work. We get our education in schools, universities and workplaces. We spend years developing our know-how and we are trained how science and technology works. These pilots were among the most experienced in Russia and they knew how to fly a plane. But knowledge is not enough for us to succeed. We need wisdom and wisdom means to build everything in life on the foundation of truth. Truth must be behind every thought, decision and action, because whenever truth is rejected, ignored, dismissed or rationalized away, something tragic is going to happen. It may take years, even decades to unfold, but the road of falsehood always ends in suffering. Everything in life must be built on the foundation of truth."

2.

"Some people believe truth is relative," I said. "Philosophers claim that truth is driven by local culture and traditions, that it depends on our individual standards of morality, or it is influenced by the social environment we live in and shaped by our upbringing and circumstances."

"Of all the things one can speak, this is likely the most stupid of all," said Theo. "Wait here."

He stepped out of the room and returned with a worn-out pocket book in his hand.

"Thirty years ago when I started my career in aviation, my supervisor opened my eyes to a simple insight that completely changed my view on life. On the day I begun working with him, he told me that before I could be responsible for the lives of thousands of passengers, I must understand one lesson hidden in this book."

Theo opened to the page where a bookmark was placed and started reading.

"In year 1633, an old man was summoned to stand trial before the Catholic Inquisition. He left his home in rural Tuscany and traveled alone the two hundred mile journey to Rome. His body was wasting under seventy years of life and every step he took demanded conscious effort. It wasn't the voyage that brought him pain, but his thoughts. It wasn't the age that crushed him, but his fear. And it wasn't the illness that pierced him, but his sorrow of heart. The seldom breaths of air he took stopped in his throat. He shriveled with dread every time the words that got him on this journey returned to his mind: "Galileo Galilei, you are suspected of heresy. You will be judged by the Holy Office for making public the false claim that the Sun is the center of the Universe and the Earth is just another planet going around the Sun. Depending on the verdict, you will be imprisoned or punished at the pleasure of the Inquisition."

Galileo arrived in Rome, got a bed in the Florentine embassy, but found no rest. He knew what the words of the letter actually meant. Five hundred years before, Pope Innocent had decreed that anyone who speaks against the Catholic church was to be burned in the public square. Many scholars have since been hoisted up to ceilings of underground dungeons, suspended with their hands tied behind their backs, iron balls dangling from their feet. Executioners sometimes dragged survivors to a scaffold in the market where they nailed their bodies to a cross. Other times they crushed their arms and legs with an iron bar and left them to die. If heretics were slow to expire, executioners strangled them and burned their bodies in public with the crowds howling around the pyre. Some of the great men of science have even been burned alive.

The following morning, Catholic priests and bishops filled the courthouse. As they murmured threats among themselves, an arm wrapped in a metal armor forced Galileo to his knees. The cardinal slammed the wooden mallet on the table and read the church's ruling: "Galileo Galilei. You have been found guilty of severe acts of heresy. The Holy Office is generous and kind, and gives you a choice: abjure your profanity or be baptized by fire in the central square of Rome. If you decide to abjure your profanity, you will abstain completely from defending this doctrine. You will abandon the opinion that the Sun is at the center of the Universe and the Earth moves around it. You will not defend this blasphemy in any way in public or in private."

Everything Galileo cherished in life — his daughter Maria Celeste and his son Vincenzo, the students at the university, his passion for astronomy and the freedom to work when everyone was sleeping, the grapes in autumn and the beers made by monks in the underground grottos of the monastery — was to be taken away from him. Galileo realized in that moment that he wasn't ready to die a torturous death for a scientific discovery. He picked up the quill and signed his name at the bottom of the scroll. On his knees, with tears in his eyes and in a trembling voice, he said to the audience: "I abjure my discovery."

Galileo stepped outside the courthouse to find the crowd already gathered in front of the door.

"What have you done, Galilei?" the crowd demanded to know.

Galileo told them the truth.

People lifted their fists and voices and snarled at him.

"Why didn't you defend your discovery?" a man shouted. "By giving in to your fear, the Inquisition triumphed again over us" he said. "Look! They even control the truth."

Galileo said nothing.

"We trusted your wisdom, Galilei. We trusted your intelligence. You have a position of honor at the university. You disappointed us," said a professor who believed in his work.

"He deceived all of us...?" questioned one of his students. "We read your books. We listened to your discourses. Was everything you taught us a lie, professor?"

Galileo looked towards the clouds floating above Rome. He then beheld the crowd and lifted his hand to quiet them and spoke. "My terror aroused the cardinal. The man stood up and walked around me in circles. I was on my knees staring at the marble floor, but I could hear the steel of his heels getting closer to me. Tears fell from my eyes like beads from a broken rosary worn out by endless pleas for mercy. The silence of the court room was the deafness of my grave."

"The cardinal and I had met several times in the past" Galileo continued. He knows me well. We exchanged letters and I admired his interest in science. He even visited me once with his wife and child at my house in Florence. His little girl loves him so much. She's not old enough to know that the same lips that kiss her in the morning speak sentences that burn people alive."

"You are a coward, Galilei!" shouted a woman from the back of the crowd.

"Please leave him alone!" cried a child in a trembling voice.

"Look at our man of truth!" yelled another student with his face disfigured in contempt.

"Do as you please... I finally told them," concluded Galileo. "And then I signed the scroll."

"You were our hope, Galileo," complained one of his friends, "but because you didn't have the courage to defend the truth, you have proven one more time that the Inquisition has power over us. They even manipulate the truth."

"No, my people," spoke Galilei and lifted again his hand to silence the crowd. "No... I merely had to choose between life and death. Going home or being burnt alive. I signed the scroll so that I can live, but this doesn't change a thing. The decision to renounce my discovery does not and cannot change the truth and the reality of things. Doesn't the Earth still spin around the Sun with me, with you, and even with my very judges and accusers? Have the words my quill left written on the scroll disturbed the movements of the sky or thrust the Earth out from its cosmic orbit?"

"Behold, you fools, the Sun is in its place! Have I, a mere man, the power to derail the planets from their course? The universe doesn't obey our madness nor what we want reality to be. Until the end of time this Earth will go around the Sun just as it spins today with my grave and your graves then swallowed in the deep. Nothing you and I do can change the great reality of things. Are you so foolish to believe that truth cares if you agree with it or not? Do you not see that truth is far beyond our preference, our desire and our will? We can discover it, study it, understand it, align our lives to it, or we can reject it, scorn at it, spit on it, turn our backs to it, but the one thing we cannot do is change it. Which one of you must now put the Earth back in its orbit because I signed the scroll just to spare my life? Or has the cardinal moved the Sun back in its place by forcing me to abjure my claim? Behold the sky again, you people and reason in yourselves. The truth just is and doesn't need to be defended as if somehow we have any word to say about it. It is not the truth that bows to people, but is us, there mere mortals, who must submit to the truth."

Theo closed the book and put it on the table.

"Truth never changes. Our understanding of the truth fluctuates from man to man and from age to age, but the truth remains constant. If something was once regarded as true but science later proved it false, then it was never true in the first place. For example, our planet was not flat for those who lived in the ancient past and then shifted form and became round. The Earth had always been the same, though our understanding of it had changed because science evolved. Science is not the truth either, as some folk believe, but only a complex set of tools to discover and understand the truth. The scientific methods accumulates observations and is supposed to draw conclusions based on the data and not to defend personal beliefs. Science is not a tool to inform one's preference for reality, but a way to discover and understand reality. Science, just like everything else in this universe, must be built on the foundation of truth."

"We won't always know what the truth is, nor will we accept it when it becomes difficult or uncomfortable to embrace. There are times in our lives when we would do anything only to avoid the truth. We can embrace it or reject it, but the truth itself exists beyond what we decide to do with it. Neither is the truth negotiable or debatable because it is above all human desire or ambition. It simply waits for us to find it, know it, embrace it and live by it if we choose to. But even when we can't grasp it or make sense of it, the truth always leaves a trail of evidence that points to it."

3.

"Speaking of truth," I interrupted Theo, "I'm in the middle of a research project to discover more of the pieces of the puzzle of the reality of Jesus Christ. One of his statements was "I am the Truth.""What do you make of it?"

"This is something I've asked myself not so long ago," he said. "Let me tell you a story."

"After Jesus was crucified, the religious people in Jerusalem fought hard against his remaining disciples to silence them. They beat them, imprisoned them and threatened to kill them if they continued to speak about Jesus. Just as the Inquisition sought to execute Galileo Galilei for what he had discovered, the Jewish leaders planned to murder the apostles of Jesus Christ for their message of salvation. In the midst of their trial, however, something dramatic happened."

Theo pulled from the drawer a worn-out Bible with blue leather covers.

"This is from *The Book of Acts*" he said and started reading.

"[The authorities] were furious and wanted to put them [the apostles] to death. But a Pharisee named Gamaliel, a teacher of the law, who was honored by all the people, stood up…and ordered that the men be put outside for a little while… "Men of Israel, he said, "consider carefully what you intend to do to these men. Some time ago there was that fellow Theudas, claiming to be someone great and about four hundred men rallied to him. He was killed, all his followers were dispersed, and it all came to nothing. After him, another fellow Judas the Galilean appeared in the days of the census and led a band of people in revolt. He too was killed and all his followers scattered. Therefore, in the present case I advise you: Leave these men alone! Let them go! For if their purpose or activity is of human origin, it will fail. But if it is from God, you will not be able to stop these men, you will only find yourselves fighting against God!"

"In a nutshell," Theo continued, "Gamaliel is saying that if Jesus Christ truly comes from God, then the number of followers will continue to grow regardless of what people believe about him. But if not, then Jesus will disappear from history like all other men before him."

Theo flipped back through the pages of the Bible. "Let's go back in ancient times."

"*The Book of Isaiah*, written about eight hundred years before Jesus Christ as a prophecy for the future, says "For unto us a child is born, of the increase of his government shall be no end." In another place, "He said, I have gathered all the earth… and you shall be gathered one by one."

"*The Book of Ezekiel*, written around 593 BC, says "For this is what the Lord GOD says: I Myself will search for My flock and seek them out…. and I will take you from the nations and gather you from all the countries."

"*The Book of Daniel*, dated somewhere between 167 - 164 BC, says: "Behold, one like the Son of Man…there was given him dominion and glory, and a kingdom that all people, nations and languages should serve him, which shall not pass away."

"*The Gospel of John* written a few decades after Christ records Jesus himself informing the crowds: "When I am lifted up from the earth, I will draw all people to myself.""

Theo drew a horizontal line on a piece of paper, and made a few marks along it.

"Look at the timeline," continued Theo.

"Around 800 BC, Isaiah envisioned that the government of the one who will come in the future will continue to grow as he will gather his people one by one. In 593 BC, Ezekiel writes that God himself will gather his people from all countries. In the 160s BC, Daniel wrote that people of all countries and languages will serve the one who is to come. In 33 AD, Jesus promised to draw all people to himself. Gamaliel then warns his fellows that if Jesus Christ truly comes from God, then regardless of their efforts, nobody will be able to stop him from fulfilling his mission."

Theo stretched forth his hand and pointed toward the sky.

"Just as the mechanics of the cosmos operate independently of and above the insanity of the Inquisition, the reality of Jesus Christ as the Son of God, if true, must be beyond any human preference. If Jesus really is the truth, then he is the truth regardless of what people believe of him. Human belief is merely the decision to accept or reject the truth, but it never has any authority or power to change the truth."

Theo pulled from his drawer a stack of hand-written documents.

"It all started with Jesus and twelve people in year 33 AD. Then, "three thousand people believed" in Jesus after apostle Peter preached to them fifty days after Christ was believed to have resurrected from the dead. Then, two thousand years later, the data speaks for itself."

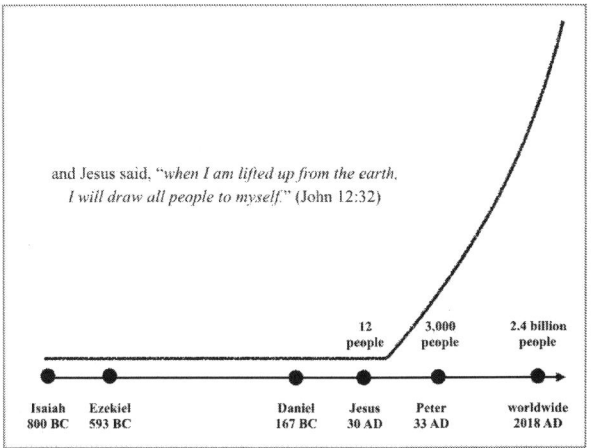

"A research study performed in 232 countries based on data recorded by the United Nations showed that in 2010 were more than 2.18 billion followers of Jesus Christ, about a third of the global population. The number of Christ followers has nearly quadrupled in the last 100 years, from 600 million in 1910 to more than 2 billion in 2010."

"The United States has by far the largest Christian population, with 71 percent of Americans - 230 million people - being followers of Jesus Christ. The Centre for the Study of Global Christianity at Gordon Conwell Theological Seminary published a study showing that the number of believers in Europe has increased by 52 percent since 1900, rising to 559 million believers in 2015.

Africa has seen a dramatic change, as the followers of Jesus Christ grew from 9 percent of the total population in 1910 to 63 percent in 2010, an increase from 9 million to 541 million people in only 100 years. Since the year 2000, African believers grew in numbers by 51 percent, which means that an average of 33,000 people per day are coming to Christ. Yale University historian Professor Lamin Sanneh commented that the growth of "African Christianity was not just an exotic, curious phenomenon in an obscure part of the world, but that African Christianity might be the shape of things to come." Scholarly research predicts that by 2025 there will be 633 million disciples of Jesus Christ in Africa. India had only 28 million Christians in 2010, but things are changing fast. One example from India is the church founded by Dr. Satish Kumar in Hyderabad. He started off with 25 people in 2005 and his congregation grew to almost 150,000 members in only ten years. The Asia-Pacific had about 28 million followers of Jesus in 1910, and numbers grew to more than 286 million in 2010. South Korea had seen its first church planted by missionaries in 1884 and in 2010 had more than 60,000 churches. China is a miracle in itself. In 1949 there were about one million Christians in China, and despite severe persecution - churches being demolished, people beaten, starved to death and tortured in Communist prisons, in 2010 there were more than 100 million Chinese followers of Jesus Christ. Dr. Fenggang Yang, Professor of Sociology at Purdue University and America's foremost authority on Christianity in China noted in 2018: "By my calculations, China is destined to become the largest Christian country in the world. It is going to happen in less than a generation and not many people are prepared for this dramatic change." Even the most conservative estimates predict that by 2030, China's total Christian population will exceed 247 million people, making it the largest Christian congregation in the world."

Theo stopped reading. "Does this evidence look as Jesus Christ drawing all people unto himself, gathering people of all languages and from every country, a mission that expands forever?"

"The data speaks by itself," I said.

"Dr. David Garrison is a church historian who has travelled more than a quarter-million miles across one hundred countries in the Muslim world," continued Theo. "In the most comprehensive research study in history documenting conversions from Islam to Christianity, Garrison discovered that since 1993 an unprecedented number of Muslims have become followers of Jesus Christ. In the Middle East in 2018 there were between 10 and 15 million followers of Christ, which is remarkable considering the fact that leaving Islam is a crime punishable by death. More and more "are willing to cast their eternity on Jesus Christ, even if that eternity begins tomorrow," noted Garrison. In his journeys he collected testimonies from children, widows, sheiks, even terrorists who became followers of Jesus Christ. Of course, anyone can believe in secret where nobody is watching, but Garrison's data included only the Muslims who made a public declaration of their faith in Jesus Christ and risked everything by being baptized in his name. Under the Islamic law, becoming a Christian is a crime that could earn them the death penalty, and their family members might be the very ones who would want to kill them."

"A 2017 study published by Pew Research Center, however, seems to contradict what Jesus Christ claimed. Because Muslim families have more babies than other faith communities, predictions are that Muslims will become the fastest-growing religious group in the decades ahead. But what the study doesn't consider is what takes place after these babies grow up and begin making choices in life. Garrison's research revealed that more Muslims have come to Christ publicly since 1993 than in the last 1,400 years of Christian missions in the Arab world. More Muslim babies might actually mean more followers of Jesus Christ. This paradigm shift correlates with the fact that since 1993 a small group of Christians began praying for the Muslim people during the Islamic month of Ramadan. Muslims pray and fast for 30 days during this month, asking Allah to speak to them. The group of Christian prayer warriors grew to hundreds of thousands of people who cry out to God on behalf of the Muslim people, asking God to reveal the truth to them. 'Is it a coincidence that 82 percent of all the Muslim conversions to Christ have occurred specifically during these same 25 years [since prayers begun]?' asked Garrison."

Theo rested back in his chair and took off his glasses.

"My research only goes so far, but there are other people out there who can guide you," he said. "Somebody once wrote that truth is that which, when you stop believing in it, doesn't go away. If you take only one thing from our conversation, remember my two stories. The truth doesn't need you. You need the truth. Build your life on the foundation of the truth because the road of error or lie ends in tragedy. I made my choice to believe in Jesus. The Bible says God gave His only Son, Jesus Christ, that whoever believes in him shall not perish but have eternal life. Your choice to believe in Jesus or not does not establish his reality, but only personal consequences. The truth doesn't change because of you. You must change according to the truth. If you are truly honest in your quest, you will find that the truth always comes out into the light and leaves a trail of evidence behind."

CHAPTER 1
The Book of Life

Q1 - What is the Bible?

"I find more sure marks of authenticity in the Bible than in any profane history whatsoever" - Sir Isaac Newton

1.

The New Testament books written by Matthew, Mark, Luke and John are the primary historical sources that describe the life and teachings of Jesus Christ. From antiquity to the present day, prestigious scholars and academics agree that the Bible is a collection of copies of historical manuscripts. The ancient writers who documented the events of gospels specifically noted they were recording real events, exactly as they took place. Luke, the author of *The Gospel of Luke*, wrote around year 60 AD that his historical narrative of the life of Jesus Christ is based on the testimony of eyewitnesses, and that he writes for others will learn "the factual account" of what took place during the ministry of Jesus. In his letter to Theophilus, Luke says that "Inasmuch as many have undertaken to compile a narrative of the things which have been accomplished among us, just as they were delivered to us by those who from the beginning were eyewitnesses and ministers of the word, it seemed good to me also, having followed all things closely for some time, to write carefully in order for you, most excellent Theophilus, that you may know the facts concerning the things of which you have been informed." Luke is "erudite, he's eloquent, his Greek approaches classical quality, he writes as an educated man," explains Dr. John McRay, professor of New Testament at Wheaton College, and he is specifically informing the reader that his document describes accurate and verifiable facts about Jesus Christ and these facts are drawn from eyewitness accounts. Another ancient writer, Justin Martyr (100 - 165 AD) concurs that the gospels are "memoirs of the apostles" that record the actual words and deeds of Jesus Christ.

Augustine of Hippo (354 - 430 AD) describes the four gospels as "trustworthy testimonies" of "the words heard from [Jesus's] lips and the deeds wrought by him beneath their eyes."

Modern academics agree that the books of the New Testament are historical biographies based on eyewitness testimonies that describe real events from the life of Jesus of Nazareth. His disciples left everything behind and lived with Jesus almost every day for three years, which offered them sufficient time to document his words and actions. Dr. Brant Pitre, distinguished professor at The Augustine Institute, writes: "There are compelling reasons for concluding that the four gospels are first-century biographies of Jesus, written within the lifetime of the apostles and based directly on eyewitness testimony. The gospels are ancient biographies. These biographies are known as 'lives' because they focus on the life of a particular person. The four gospels are not just any kind of ancient biography. They are historical biographies, two of which explicitly claim to tell us what Jesus actually did and said."

Dr. Richard Burridge of King's College London, in his academic book *What Are the Gospels?* demonstrates that the manuscripts of the Bible were read as biographies in the first centuries after Jesus Christ and belong to the recognized literary genre of historical biographies. Dr. Graham Stanton, professor of New Testament at King's College London confirms that "early Christian readers of the gospels did read them as biographies." The gospels are not a collection of ancient stories and myths, but rather actual eyewitness testimonies documented and written down by knowledgable and educated people. The disciples of Jesus Christ sent letters to the early believers to confirm they had witnessed the events they wrote about. Peter writes in his epistle that "we were not making up clever stories when we told you about the powerful coming of our Lord Jesus Christ. We saw his majestic splendor with our own eyes." John says, "we proclaim to you what we ourselves have actually seen and heard so that you may have fellowship with us." *The Gospel of John* declares that "this report is from an eyewitness giving an accurate account," and Luke writes in *Acts* that "we cannot stop telling about everything we have seen and heard."

How accurate and reliable are the New Testament gospels?

Contemporary scholars agree with remarkable unanimity that the New Testament manuscripts attest to the actual life and teachings of Jesus Christ. In light of the chronicled evidence, Dr. Benjamin Warfield, distinguished professor at Princeton Theological Seminary, writes: "If we compare the present state of the New Testament text with that of any other ancient writing, we must declare it to be marvelously correct. Such has been the care with which the New Testament has been copied. The New Testament [is] unrivaled among ancient writings in the purity of its text as actually transmitted and kept in use." Scholars Dr. Norman Geisler and Dr. William Nix concur to the authenticity and accuracy of the gospel manuscripts: "The New Testament has not only survived in more manuscripts than any other book from antiquity, but it has survived in a purer form than any other great book - a form that is 99.5 percent pure."

Scholars have tested again and again the reliability of the scriptures using the same rigorous criteria that apply to all historical documents and concluded that the gospels of the New Testament are the most accurate documents in ancient history. "If I were to remain intellectually honest," writes Josh McDowell, a skeptic who investigated the historicity of the Bible and then dedicated the next 50 years of his life to preaching the gospel of Jesus Christ, "I had to admit that the Old and New Testament documents are the most reliable writings in all of antiquity."

Critics claim that the first manuscripts of the New Testament had been written some hundreds of years after the events took place, but modern scholarly research proves that the gospels were in fact recorded in the immediate years following the crucifixion of Jesus Christ. Dr. William F. Albright, the world's foremost authority on biblical archaeology, notes that "there is no longer any solid basis for dating any book of the New Testament after about 80 AD. In my opinion, every book of the New Testament was written by a baptized Jew between the forties and the eighties of the first century AD, probably sometime between about 50 and 75 AD." Scholar Dr. John A. T. Robinson found in his research that most books of the New Testament were written before the destruction of the temple in Jerusalem in 70 AD. Dr. Gary Habermas, distinguished professor at Liberty University proved that some of the earliest New Testament documents have actually been written as close as one to two years after the crucifixion of Jesus Christ. British scholar James D.G. Dunn, professor at the University of Durham noted that the words and deeds of Jesus Christ have been memorized and recorded by his early followers as early as six months after the crucifixion, a finding that even professor Bart D. Ehrman, America's foremost skeptic agrees with considering the available historical data.

In judging the authority of the New Testament manuscripts, the wealth of catalogued material is overwhelming in comparison to other ancient texts. The New Testament has been preserved in more manuscripts than any other ancient work of literature, with more than 5,850 complete or fragmented Greek manuscripts, 10,000 Latin manuscripts and 9,300 manuscripts in other ancient languages. Gary Habermas comments that "the New Testament has far more manuscript evidence from a far earlier period than other classical works. There are just under 6,000 [catalogued] New Testament manuscripts, with copies dating from just 100 years or so after its writing. [Other] classical sources almost always have fewer than 20 copies each and usually date from 700 - 1400 years after the composition of the work." Historian Stephen Neill notes that "we have a far better and more reliable text of the New Testament than of any other ancient work." Scholars agree that there are more New Testament manuscripts copied with greater accuracy and earlier dating than any secular classic writing from antiquity. Dr. Craig Blomberg, professor of New Testament at Denver Seminary, explains that the texts of the New Testament "have been preserved in far greater number and with much more care than have any other ancient documents." He confirms that "97–99% of the New Testament can be reconstructed beyond any reasonable doubt." Greek scholar J. Harold Greenlee also comments that "the reliability of the text of the New Testament is assured." Dr. Daniel B. Wallace, professor of New Testament at Dallas Theological Seminary noted that "New Testament scholars face an embarrassment of riches compared to the data the classical Greek and Latin scholars have to contend with. The average classical author's literary remains number no more than twenty copies. We have more than 1,000 times the manuscript data for the New Testament" than we do for the average antiquity authors. Biblical scholar Dr. F. F. Bruce notes that "the evidence for our New Testament writings is ever so much greater than the evidence for many writings of classical authors, the authenticity of which no one dreams of questioning. And if the New Testament were a collection of secular writings, their authenticity would generally be regarded as beyond all doubt." Sir Frederic G. Kenyon, who was a British paleographer and biblical scholar, president of the British Academy and director of the British Museum, dedicated his entire life to studying the historicity of the New Testament documents. He writes, "The interval then between the dates of original composition and the earliest extant evidence becomes so small as to be in fact negligible, and the last foundation for any doubt that the Scriptures have come down to us substantially as they were written has now been removed. Both the authenticity and the general integrity of the books of the New Testament may be regarded as finally established."

Is there any external evidence about the New Testament gospels?

Despite the historical evidence and the authority of the manuscripts of the gospels, critics may still question their veracity. Jesus's followers could have written the New Testament scrolls and others might have copied them with great accuracy, but these documents alone do not necessarily make Jesus Christ a historical figure, let alone the Son of God. Therefore, one must question if are there historical documents outside the Bible that confirm the testimony of the gospels.

Papias (60 - 163 AD) learned directly from those who have been in the presence of the apostles. He writes, "I made enquiries about the words of the elders — what Andrew or Peter had said, or Philip or Thomas or James or John or Matthew or any other of the Lord's disciples, and whatever Aristion and John the Elder, the Lord's disciples, were saying. For I did not think that information from the books would profit me as much as information from a living and surviving voice." Papias continues to shed light on how the gospels were written. "The Elder [apostle John] used to say this also: "Mark, having been the interpreter of Peter, wrote down accurately all that he mentioned, whether sayings or doings of Christ, not, however, in order. So then Mark made no mistake, writing down in this way some things as he mentioned them; for he paid attention to this one thing, not to omit anything that he had heard, not to include any false statement among them."

Polycarp (69 - 156 AD), who had been the disciple of apostle John, taught his student Iraneus: "Matthew published his gospel among the Hebrews in their own tongue when Peter and Paul were preaching the gospel in Rome and founding the church there. After their departure [i.e. death, around year 64 AD], Mark, the disciple and interpreter of Peter, himself handed down to us in writing the substance of Peter's preaching. Luke, the follower of Paul, set down in a book the gospel preached by his teacher. Then John, the disciple of the Lord, who also leaned on his breast himself produced his gospel, while he was living at Ephesus in Asia."

Iraneus (130 - 202 AD) writes in a letter to his fellow Florinus his memories of Polycarp, his spiritual father: "I could tell you the place where the blessed Polycarp sat to preach the Word of God. I seem to hear him now relate how he conversed with John and many others who had seen Jesus Christ, the words he had heard from their mouths."

In *The Historical Jesus: Ancient Evidence for the Life of Christ,* Dr. Gary Habermas presents evidence for Jesus Christ, including Greek, Roman and Jewish manuscripts that confirm the crucifixion of Jesus by the Romans, the early followers worshipping Jesus as God, and their belief in the bodily resurrection of Jesus Christ. Habermas concludes that "ancient extra-biblical sources do present a surprisingly large amount of detail concerning both the life of Jesus and the nature of early Christianity." The earliest writings outside the Bible are clear and unanimous about the factuality of the New Testament accounts. Ancient non-biblical writers not only confirm that the gospels are authentic historical documents, but they also bring independent corroboration to confirm their testimony. Historian Irenaeus points out in his work *Against Heresies* that immediately after Jesus Christ was crucified, various groups had already begun picking from the gospels only the teachings convenient to them and scraping the rest, nonetheless thus testifying to their historical reality. He writes, "So firm is the ground upon which these gospels rest that the very heretics themselves bear witness to them, and starting from these [documents] each one of them endeavors to establish his own peculiar doctrine."

Tacitus was a Roman senator and one of the most important historians of the Roman empire. In 115 AD, he documented the most factual proof about Jesus Christ outside the Bible. He wrote that emperor Nero persecuted the followers of Jesus as scapegoats to divert the public suspicion from himself for the fire that destroyed Rome in year 64 AD. Tacitus writes: "Nero fastened the guilt and inflicted the most exquisite tortures on a class hated for their abominations called Christians by the populace. Christus, from whom the name had its origin, suffered the extreme penalty during the reign of Tiberius at the hands of one of our procurators, Pontius Pilatus."

Professor F. F. Bruce comments that "some writers may toy with the fancy of a 'Christ-myth,' but they do not do so on the ground of historical evidence. The historicity of [Jesus] Christ is as axiomatic for an unbiased historian as the historicity of Julius Caesar."

Even historical documents written by the very enemies of Christianity corroborate and confirm the claims of the gospels, according to which Jesus Christ was worshipped as God. One of these sources comes from Pliny the Younger whose correspondence with the Roman emperor Trajan is preserved until present day. In 111 AD, Pliny writes about the persecution he inflicted on the disciples of Jesus: "I have asked them if they are Christians and if they admit it I repeat the question a second and third time with a warning of the punishment awaiting them. If they persist, I order them to be led away for execution, for whatever the nature of their admission I am convinced that their stubbornness and unshakable obstinacy ought not to go unpunished…the sum total of their guilt or error amounted to no more than this: they had met regularly before dawn on a fixed day to chant verses […] in honor of Christ, as if to a god, and also to bind themselves by oath … to abstain from theft, robbery, adultery. This made me decide it was all the more necessary to extract the truth by torture from two slave women, whom they called deaconesses. I found nothing but a degenerate sort of cult carried to extravagant lengths."

British academic A. N. Sherwin-White writes about the *The Book of Acts* that "the confirmation of [its] historicity is overwhelming. Any attempt to reject its basic historicity even in matters of detail must now appear absurd. Roman historians have long taken it for granted." Josephus, one of the most important first century Romano-Jewish historians, writes about James the brother of Jesus who was executed in year 62 AD: "Now [Ananus] assembled the Sanhedrin of judges and brought before them the brother of Jesus, who was called Christ, whose name was James, and some others; and when he had formed an accusation against them as breakers of the law, he delivered them to be stoned."

"The New Testament is better attested by ancient manuscripts than any other piece of ancient literature," notes Dr. Douglas Groothuis, professor of philosophy at Denver Seminary. Modern science and academic research proves with solid data that the gospels are historical biographies based on eyewitness accounts. Scholars demonstrate that regardless of their content, the New Testament manuscripts are the most pure, reliable and accurate ancient documents in the history of humanity. External sources, some written by the very persecutors of Christianity, confirm the historical reliability of the gospels. Dr. Brant Pitre of The Augustine Institute concludes: "[The Gospels] are ancient biographies written by the students of Jesus and their followers, written well within the lifetimes of the apostles and eyewitnesses of Jesus. As such, they provide us with a sound basis for investigating the historical questions of what Jesus did, what he said and who he claimed to be." Therefore, the question is what do eyewitnesses testify about Jesus Christ?

2.

What do the gospels declare about Jesus Christ?

Professor C.S. Lewis summarized in one sentence the importance of Jesus Christ in the history of humanity. He says, "Christianity, if false, is of no importance, and if true, of infinite importance." There are no options in between. Christianity is founded on the fact that God, the Creator of the universe, was born and walked the earth in the person of Jesus Christ, he died crucified as an atonement for our sins and was resurrected after three days to eternal life. If Jesus was a mere teacher, then Christianity is but another philosophy. But if Jesus is, in fact, God, this very reality and his teachings are of absolute importance for every person who lives on this planet.

The New Testament gospels tell us that Jesus himself claimed to be God and also demonstrated this statement through his actions. He revealed his identity as God through demonstrations of power, miracles, signs and wonders. He "healed all the sick," "cast out devils" and set people free from demonic oppression, and even raised the dead back to life. People "begged him to let the sick touch at least the fringe of his robe and all who touched him were healed." Jesus "saw the huge crowd and he had compassion on them and healed their sick." The New Testament also documents Jesus publicly raising several people from the dead, including a twelve-year-old girl who had just died, a boy who was being carried in his coffin on the way to the grave, and a man who had been buried four days before. The manuscripts also record Jesus casting out demons from people in front of the crowds. Jesus Christ claimed to be God and demonstrated his words with miracles and wonders "done among them which no one else did." Dr. E.P. Sanders, professor at Duke University, regards it as an "almost indisputable" historical fact that "Jesus was a Galilean who preached and healed." Using traditional historical-critical tools, John Meier of the University of Notre Dame found that many of Jesus's reported miracles are authentic.

The Trial of Jesus Christ

Throughout history, people from various cultures and traditions pointed the way to God, wrote about God, instructed about God, but none ever claimed to be God and confirmed their words with miracles and wonders. Psychotic individuals can declare to be God, but they cannot heal the sick, raise the dead to life, cast out demons, nor speak wisdom that heals the broken hearted. Jesus, however, stated it perfectly clear that he was the only Son of God, born before the foundation of the world, of the same nature with God, sent into this world as a sacrifice for our sin, and the only way for people to come into the presence of God and receive eternal life. Jesus left no room for doubt about who he claimed to be and for this very reason the Jewish authorities condemned him to death. *The Gospel of Mark* documents his trial:

"Again, the high priest asked him, "Are you the Christ, the Son of God?" And Jesus said, "I Am, and you will see the Son of Man seated at the right hand of Power and coming with the clouds of heaven." And the high priest tore his garments and said, "Why do we still need witnesses? You have heard his blasphemy…And they all condemned him as deserving death."

Jesus answered the questions of his accusers in the context of the first century Judea by making reference to the Jewish scriptures written hundreds of years before him. In *The Book of Daniel*, the Son of Man is portrayed as coming on the clouds of a heaven and *The Book of Psalms* reveals him as the Son of God born before everything was created and as Lord seated at the right hand of God.

"Behold, with the clouds of heaven there came one like *a Son of Man*
and he came to the Ancient of Days,
and was presented before him,
and to him was given dominion and glory and kingdom,
that all peoples, nations and languages
should serve him;
his dominion is an everlasting dominion,
which shall not pass away, and his kingdom one
that shall not be destroyed." (*The Book of Daniel*)

"The LORD says to my Lord:
Sit at my right hand, til I make your enemies your footstool.
…From the womb of dawn, like the dew I have begotten you." (*The Book of Psalms*)

By referring to himself as the Son of Man, Jesus indicates that although he appears to have the appearance of a mere human, he comes from heaven, enters the presence of God at will, he is seated at the right hand of God, and the entire world had been given to him for eternity.

The Crucifixion of Jesus Christ

Although he has never hurt anyone nor has he done any evil, after an illegal trial held at the flames of burning torches in the late hours of the night, the Jewish authorities condemned Jesus to death. Several men hit him with their fists, spat in his face, then dragged him tied in ropes to be flogged and crucified. The Roman soldiers stripped the clothes off Jesus and tied his hands above his head to a pole. Using whips made of leather thongs with metal balls and sharp fragments of bone interwoven in them, the soldiers lashed him, with orders to bring him close to death. The metal balls produced lacerations in his body, and the leather cords shredded his back and legs to the point where his skin and muscles were hanging in strips of raw flesh. The bone fragments impaled his body and tore his flesh to shreds when the soldiers pulled out the whips. The Roman floggings were so heinous that "the veins were laid bare, and the very muscles, sinews and bowels of the victim were open to exposure," wrote ancient historian Eusebius. By the time the flogging was over, Jesus had collapsed in his own blood in the dust. The Roman soldiers then twisted boughs from some bushes covered in spines, made a crown of thorns and thrust it on his head. Unlike the crown depicted in paintings, the real one might have covered his entire scalp. Soldiers spat on Jesus and struck his head with a wooden staff thus impaling the thorns further into his scalp and forehead. Blood from his head gushed on his face, into his eyes and ears, and down on his neck to the point where "his appearance was so disfigured beyond that of any human being, and his form marred beyond human likeness."

Crucifixion was a form of torture and capital punishment devised to inflict the slowest possible death with excruciating suffering. Romans exerted it only on slaves, murderers, military deserters and the worst criminals. Historians of the time observed that crucifixion was "the most wretched of deaths," and "the most severe punishment possible." Historian Flavius Josephus wrote of the hundreds of Jewish prisoners crucified in Jerusalem in 70 AD: "They were first whipped and then tormented with all sorts of tortures, before they died, and were crucified before the wall of the city…the soldiers, out of wrath and hatred they bore the Jews, nailed those they caught to the crosses in different postures." Seneca the Younger, a Roman philosopher contemporary of Jesus Christ, documented another mass crucifixion. He writes, "I see crosses there, not just of one kind but made in many different ways: some have their victims with their head down to the ground, some impale their private parts, others stretch out their arms." In another document, Seneca notes, "Can anyone be found who would prefer wasting away in pain, dying limb by limb, or letting out his life drop by drop, rather than expiring once for all? Can any man be found willing to be fastened to the accursed tree, long sickly, already deformed, swelling with ugly tumors on chest and shoulders, and draw the breath of life amid long-drawn-out agony?"

Aftey they flogged him, soldiers pulled Jesus from the dust, placed a large beam of wood weighting about a hundred pounds on his shredded shoulders, outstretched his hands and fastened them with ropes, and forced him into the street. Jesus slogged through one of the main roads of Jerusalem in the eyes of the multitudes who were "appalled to look at him." The crowd howled, witnesses spat on him, thumped him, lifted their fits and voices to curse him, while soldiers continued to lash him with their whips. His mother was pressing through the crowd in tears, trying to reach his son who was carrying the cross to his death. Women wailed in the street and soldiers continued to strike him. The flogging had been so fierce that his internal organs begun to fail and Jesus collapsed on the cobblestone pavement. Because his hands were stretched and tied to the horizontal crossbeam, he couldn't break the fall which produced a contusion of the heart, "predisposing his heart to rupture on the cross," as modern medical researchers who studied the crucifixion wrote. He was pulled up by the soldiers, but then collapsed two more times to the ground before a man was forced to carry his crossbeam to the crucifixion site.

Once there, the soldiers ripped his clothes together with flesh off his shredded body and threw Jesus on the ground with his bare back in the dust. They pulled his arms again along the wooden crossbar. A soldier probably then stepped on his arm to lock it into place and hammered a seven-inch wrought-iron nail through his wrist, into the wood. He then moved to the other arm and repeated the strike. Paintings of the crucifixion portray Jesus pierced through his palms, but the Romans actually crucified people through their wrists. If the nails had been driven through his palms, the weight of his body would have torn the skin and bones, and Jesus would have fallen off the cross. The iron nails crushed several nerves, causing fierce pain and clenching his hands like claws. Soldiers then extended Jesus's legs and hammered the nail through the bones of his feet pressed against each other. When executioners lifted the cross in vertical position, Jesus's body sagged under its weight and his elbows and shoulders dislocated. His mother was standing at the foot of the cross. Passersby mocked and cursed him, and the Roman soldiers cast lots for his clothing. His blood was draining down on the cross into the stoney ground. Jesus's chest muscles paralyzed and his arms held up and outward locked the ribcage in the inspiratory position, which made it almost impossible for him to exhale. In order to breathe, Jesus had to push himself upward in the nail in his feet, gasp for a breath, and then let his body fall with his shredded back against the wood of the cross. He could gasp only shallow breaths, which is why he uttered just a few words on the cross. The gospels document his last statements. Jesus looked at the Roman soldiers and prayed for them, saying,"Father, forgive them, for they do not know what they do." He then spoke to the repentant criminal who had been crucified next to him and repented, "Truly I tell you, today you will be with me in paradise." Then Jesus cried out: "My God, my God, why have you forsaken me?"

Since the first scribes put the quill on papyrus to write the earliest manuscripts of the gospels, even the most devoted followers of Jesus Christ did not know what to make of his last words on the cross, "My God, my God, why have you forsaken me?" It seems that the God in which he believed his whole life had abandoned him at the hour of his greatest need, and Jesus died in despair. Critics have used these words to demonstrate that after all, Jesus Christ wasn't the Son of God because he didn't save himself from the cross and in the end was abandoned by God. Throughout his life, however, Jesus spoke about himself only by making reference to the ancient Jewish scriptures and his final words must also be understood in the first-century context. "In ancient Judaism" notes Dr. Brant Pitre, "it was customary to invoke an entire psalm just by quoting the first line." The last words of Jesus Christ are the first verse of Psalm 22 from King David's *Book of Psalms:*

"My God, my God, why have you forsaken me?
   Why are you so far from saving me,
   so far from my cries of anguish?

… Dogs surround me,
a pack of villains encircles me;
they pierced my hands and my feet."

This psalm was written more than one thousand years before Jesus Christ as a prophecy for the future generations. It begins with the desperate cry of a person being crucified, "they pierced my hands and my feet," and continues to reveal what will unfold on the earth following this event:

"…All the ends of the earth
   will remember and turn to the Lord,
and all the families of the nations
   will bow down before him,
for dominion belongs to the Lord
   and he rules over the nations.
All the rich of the earth will feast and worship;
   all who go down to the dust will kneel before him,
Posterity will serve him;
   future generations will be told about the Lord.
They will proclaim his righteousness,
   declaring to a people yet unborn:
   He has done it!"

Regarded in the Jewish context of first-century Judea, Jesus's seeming cry of despair was in fact his shout of victory, as "all the ends of the earth will remember and turn to the Lord" and "all the families of the nations will bow down before him" and future generations will learn about the Lord, who is Christ Jesus, the Son of Man seated at the right hand of God. The psalm begins with his crucifixion, but ends with the entire world bowing before him in worship.

The Death of Jesus Christ

Modern medical research found that crucifixion victims can survive between two and four days nailed to the cross. Jesus, however, died in only six hours. Romans had crucified thousands of people before Jesus and were familiar with how long a person can survive on the cross, which explains why "Pilate was surprised to hear that he was already dead" when a follower requested his body after six hours. *The Gospel of John* documents a conversation between Jesus and his disciples one day before he was crucified. Jesus said to them, "I lay down my life in order to take it up again. No one takes it from me, but I lay it down of my own accord." The following day after six hours on the cross, "Jesus cried out again with a loud voice and yielded up His spirit," which seems to reveal that his death occurred by Jesus giving himself up at will, just as he had said the day before.

When Jesus died, the New Testament records a great darkness coming upon the face of the earth for three hours and an earthquake in the region. "From noon until three in the afternoon darkness came over all the land. The earth shook, the rocks split and the tombs broke open" documents *The Gospel of Matthew*. This improbable celestial event seems to turn the gospels into myths. Non-biblical manuscripts however, although hostile to Christianity, emerged in the same time with the gospels and confirm the earthquake and the inexplicable darkness. Historian Julius Africanus quotes Greek scholar Thallus who wrote in 52 AD about a darkness that occurred in the same time with the crucifixion of Jesus. He says, "On the whole world there pressed a most fearful darkness; and the rocks were rent by an earthquake, and many places in Judea and other districts were thrown down." Phlegon of Tralles wrote in his compendium *Olympiads*: "In the

4th year of the 202nd Olympiad, there was a great eclipse of the sun, greater than had ever been known before, for at the 6th hour the day was changed into night and the stars were seen in the heavens. An earthquake occurred in Bythinia and overthrew a great part of the city of Nicaea." Phlegon tried to explain away the darkness as a full eclipse of the sun, but eclipses can cause darkness for only a few minutes, not for three hours. Moreover, Jesus was crucified during the Jewish festival of Passover, and Passovers only take place during the full moon when an eclipse is impossible because the earth is exactly between the Sun and the moon. Phlegon's chronicle also confirms the year of Jesus's crucifixion. The 202nd Olympiad took place between July 29 AD and June 33 AD, and according to Phlegon, the darkness was in the forth year, therefore pointing at the year 33 AD for the crucifixion of Jesus.

Origen of Alexandra writes in his book *Against Celsus* "with regard to the eclipse in the time of Tiberius Caesar in whose reign Jesus appears to have been crucified and the great earthquakes which then took place." Tertullian, a prolific author who was named "the founder of Western theology" wrote to the Romans in 197 AD that the darkness was recorded in their official Roman government archives. He says, "At the same time at noonday there was a great darkness. They thought it to be an eclipse, who did not know that this was also foretold concerning Christ. And yet you have that remarkable events in your archive." Historian Eusebius wrote, "Jesus Christ underwent his passion in the 18th year of Tiberius (33 AD). Also at that time, in another Greek compendium, we find an event recorded in these words: the Sun was eclipsed, Bithynia was struck by an earthquake and in the city of Nicaea many buildings fell."

The U.S. National Oceanic and Atmospheric Administration agency has an extensive database of earthquakes recorded throughout history around the world. NOAA also catalogued an earthquake in year 33 AD that occurred in Palestine, the land where Jesus was crucified. Several other geological studies published in scientific journals also confirmed that a significant earthquake took place in the region around Jerusalem in the year 33 AD. These non-Biblical sources confirm the statements of the gospels according to which an earthquake shook the land and an unusual darkness came upon the face of the earth for three hours when Jesus Christ breathed his last. His death, however, was only the beginning.

The Risen Jesus Christ

The New Testament documents state that after his death, Jesus Christ appeared alive in bodily form to his disciples as well as to his persecutors several times. The first to see the risen Jesus were Mary Magdalene, Mary the mother of James and Salome. Three days after he was buried, the three women bought spices to the tomb to anoint his body when Jesus appeared to them on the road. "Greetings," he said. They came to him, clasped his feet and worshiped him. Then Jesus said to them, "Do not be afraid. Go and tell my brothers to go to Galilee. There they will see me." Mary then went and told the disciples who were mourning and weeping that Jesus is alive, but they didn't believe her. Days later, Jesus appeared to his disciples as they were eating. "He rebuked them for their lack of faith and their stubborn refusal to believe those who had seen him after he had risen." In *The Epistle to Corinthians*, Paul documents several other appearances of Jesus Christ after his death. He writes, "[Jesus] appeared to Cephas and then to the twelve. After that, he appeared to more than five hundred of the brothers and sisters at the same time, most of whom are still living, though some have fallen asleep. Then he appeared to James, then to all the apostles, and last of all he appeared to me also. For I am the least of the apostles… because I persecuted the church of God."

Before he was crucified, Jesus told people several times, "I have come down from heaven. I came from the Father and entered the world, now I am leaving the world and going back to the Father who is in heaven." After his crucifixion, the Bible describes several other occasions in which "Jesus presented himself alive after his passion by many proofs, appearing to them during forty days and speaking of the kingdom of God." Then Jesus "led them out as far as Bethany, and he lifted up his hands and blessed them. While he was blessing them, he parted from them and was carried up into heaven. He was received up into heaven and sat down at the right hand of God."

Jesus Christ declared to be God. Eyewitnesses testify that Jesus did not only reveal his divinity by referring to the ancient Jewish scriptures, but he also confirmed his words through miracles that only God could perform. He publicly healed the sick, cast out demons and raised the dead to life in front of the astonished crowds. He was "hated for no reason," brutally beaten and crucified as a sacrifice for the sin of humanity. He died, was buried and then appeared alive to his disciples and hundreds of other people in bodily form several times after his death. Jesus then sent his disciples to the ends of the earth to "preach the kingdom of God, heal the sick, cast out demons and raise the dead" themselves. He ascended into heaven to be at the right hand of God forever.

If the Jesus Christ who died by crucifixion is the same person who was raised from the dead, then several extraordinary questions emerge. If Jesus is "alive forever and ever" as the Bible declares, does Jesus still heal the sick today? Does he still cast out demons, bind up the brokenhearted and raise the dead back to life in our modern world? Does Jesus still appear to people in bodily form? Is Jesus Christ in heaven? Can modern science provide answers to these questions based on actual evidence and not on religious beliefs? The following chapters investigate through the eyes of science several pieces of the greatest puzzle humanity is yet to solve: the mystery of the reality of Jesus Christ.

CHAPTER 2

If You Can Only Believe

Q2 - Does Jesus heal the sick today?

"I am bound to be true." - Abraham Lincoln

1.

The gospel writers documented that Jesus frequently healed the sick. *The Gospel of Matthew* recalls that Jesus "healed all the sick among them." People "begged him to let the sick touch at least the fringe of his robe and all who touched him were healed." In another account, "Jesus saw the huge crowd and he had compassion on them and healed their sick." Often, "great crowds came to him, bringing the lame, the blind, the crippled, the mute and many others, and laid them at his feet and he healed them." Historical chronicles record not only that "Jesus healed them all," but he also sent his disciples to "heal the sick" themselves. Jesus publicly stated that, "unless you people see signs and wonders, you will never believe" that he really is the Son of God and the Savior of the world. In fact, he insisted "do not believe me unless I do the works of my Father. But if I do them, even though you do not believe me, believe the works." If Jesus and his disciples had indeed healed the sick during their time on earth, and if Jesus Christ is alive today as the gospels proclaim, then does Jesus and his disciples still heal the sick today? Can modern science provide an answer to this question?

Until mid 1900s, Christian evangelists focused solely on preaching the gospel of Jesus Christ and were not too concerned about the medical evidence skeptics demanded of them. Those looking to discredit the miraculous healings proclaimed by ministers often stated there is no medical documentation to support their claims and therefore must be false. Times and ways of thinking changed and in the 1950s, in an effort to fit into the modern culture driven by science, ministers started collecting medical evidence for the healing miracles reported in their services.

Kathryn Kuhlman, one the most respected Christian leaders of the twentieth century, begun gathering medical data after a reporter, Emily Gardiner Neal, performed a thorough investigation on her ministry and wrote an article titled *Can Faith in God Heal the Sick?* Neal examined the miracles in Kuhlman's ministry, collected medical evidence, hospital records, eyewitness testimonies and proof letters from those who claimed to have been healed. By the time she finished her research, Neal converted to Christianity convinced that many people have been healed by God during Kathryn Kuhlman's church services. "I came to scoff, but remained to pray," wrote Neal who later begun her own healing ministry in the name of Jesus Christ.

Kuhlman often reminded people that God has "the power to heal instantly without the material tools of scientific medicine," but she also concurred that God often works through physicians to heal. "If you are ill and have not yet received the gift of faith so that you believe in miracles, then get yourself the best medical assistance possible and pray that God shall work through the human vessel. Pray that your doctor will be given divine guidance in treating you and then both of you wait for God to do the actual healing," Kuhlman instructed people.

One of the many documented cases is Evelyn Harper. She had developed a rare kind of arthritis and doctors told her that she will not have another day of sound health for the rest of her life. For twenty-nine years she had suffered pain in every joint and muscle in her body and terrible headaches. "I believed God could do anything" Evelyn confessed, "but I was never taught to expect healing for myself." Her twin daughters Jeanne and Joan fell pray to the same illness. One of them was regularly lying in bed sixteen hours a day and couldn't lift her baby, and her sister was not able to even hold a jar of peanut butter without supporting her hand with the other arm. When the daughters bought bus tickets for the three of them to attend a Kathryn Kuhlman meeting, Evelyn refused to go because she didn't believe miracles could happen to them. She changed her mind after a few days for the only reason, however, not to lose the money spent on bus fares. When they arrived at the auditorium they found ten thousand people inside praising and worshipping Jesus Christ. Evelyn and her daughters only found seats in the upper balcony and had to use binoculars to be able to see Kathryn Kuhlman on the platform. Kuhlman didn't lay hands or anyone nor did she pray for the people. She had been preaching for a while when all of a sudden she stopped in the middle of the sentence, pointed her finger toward the place where the three women were seated and said "There's been three spinal healings in the upper balcony. Would you please stand up and receive your healing?" Without exchanging looks or talking to each other, Evelyn and her daughters simultaneously stood up. Whey they got up, the pain and the sufferings they had endured for so many years had been instantly healed. Evelyn and her daughters appeared together on public television and testified about their miraculous healing.

Kathryn Kuhlman regarded medical data as yet another instrument to open the minds and hearts of people to the reality of Jesus Christ. Her team documented decades of healing testimonies and Kuhlman presented sixty of these cases in her books *I Believe in Miracles* (1962), *God Can Do It Again* (1969) and *Nothing Is Impossible with God* (1974). She often encouraged people to verify the miracles and document their healing at the hospital. Kuhlman described in her books only the miracle cases that met a strict set of criteria, including: the healing had to have occurred rapidly, often instantly, involving changes that could not easily be explained as psychosomatic or naturally healed; the patient's medical doctor documented the healing in official hospital records; the healing had occurred long enough in the past not to be diagnosed as natural healing or remission. She recorded instant healings of debilitating, life-threatening conditions, such as recoveries from terminal cancer, regeneration and reappearance of decayed tissues, bones growing back, recovery from paralysis, healing from multiple sclerosis, instant deliverance from alcohol and drug addiction, and blind eyes regaining sight. One of these cases was a man blind for twenty-one years as the result of a piece of molten steel burning his eye in a factory who regained sight during a service. Doctors measured his blind eye the following day and found it to be 85 percent normal. Seventeen years later, his eyes were still healthy. All sixty cases Kuhlman described in her books are backed by medical data from major U.S. medical centers.

Similar to the great majority of Christian ministers, Kuhlman frequently insisted that she was not a faith healer, but the healer is God. "I have nothing to do with these healings," she often told her audiences. "I have only yielded my life to Jesus Christ. Do not try to reach out and touch Kathryn Kuhlman. Reach up and touch Jesus!"

Delores Winder was one of the hundreds of thousands of people who attended Kathryn Kuhlman's services. Suffering from a rare disease that was causing her bones to become brittle, she had lived in a bodycast for nearly fifteen years. She had suffered four spinal fusions and other surgeries so brutal they had since been forbidden by modern medicine. "Doctors go to the back of the brain and burn the nerve centers so that you can never feel again," she remembered in an interview for public television. Delores had no physical sensation from the neck down on the right side of the body and no feeling from the waist down on the left. Her husband Bill recalls her often pounding her fists on the house walls, crying "Lord, why don't you take me?" She loved God but she didn't believe God still heals. One day when she was lying in bed, the mother of the housekeeper turned on the television and Kathryn Kuhlman came on with her miracle services. Delores commanded her to turn it off. "I was always told that Kathryn Kuhlman was a cook, that her healings were not true and I believed what people have told me" she confessed. Her doctor, who was also personal friend of the family, did everything he could, but Delores' heart and lungs were in critical condition and her kidneys begun to close off.

On August 30, 1975, two weeks after she had made all the arrangements for her funeral, Delores finally agreed to attend a conference on the Holy Spirit in Dallas, Texas, where Kathryn Kuhlman was speaking. When Kuhlman walked on stage, Delores remembers thinking in herself, *Dear God, I cannot stand to look at her!* She decided to leave in the middle of the service because she considered that Kathryn Kuhlman was putting on a show. She started moving towards the edge of the seat when suddenly she felt her feet burning as if on fire. Some man helped her up and they started walking together towards the exit door. They took a few steps on the isle when the man suddenly told her, "You can take your bodycast off if you want to," to which Delores recalls thinking, *Dear God, these people are dangerous.* "Do you want to take it off?" the man asked her one more time. "I have been in one of these for fifteen years and I'm dying," she answered him. Nonetheless, she agreed to remove her cast and carried it up on the platform where Kuhlman was speaking. Delores begun walking by herself and sensations returned to her legs. She was in shock because she couldn't believe what was happening to her. Nevertheless, it was happening. Several minutes later she walked and then ran across the platform in front of three thousand people. For the first time in her life she touched the floor with her hands. She was completely healed. After fifteen years of illness, Delores said "it took only fifteen minutes for God to release me from all the chains of bondage and sickness." That evening her adopted son witnessed her walking by herself for the first time in his life. She called her physician the following day, who confessed that he was expecting a phone call from her husband telling him that Delores had died. "This is truly a miracle from God," the doctor told her, "and you have work to do for Him." Delores lived until a very old age.

Kathryn Kuhlman also included in her books medical cases for which psychosomatic or natural explanations are impossible. She documented healings of infants and children suffering from congenital bone deformities, hydrocephalus, epilepsy and blood diseases. One of these cases was of a four-month old baby born with a dislocated hip. The baby was the child of Dr. Richard Owellen, medical doctor and professor at John Hopkins University. After seeing his baby's leg straighten by itself, Owellen confessed, "I had often wondered if many of the healings I had seen weren't psychosomatic, but a four-month old baby [with a dislocated hip] doesn't know enough to have psychosomatic healing."

Kuhlman welcomed medical doctors and experts to investigate the miracles claims in her ministry. Dr. Richard Casdorph, M.D., research scientist and cardiologist at the Mayo Clinic and professor at the University of California Medical School, reviewed the medical data of tens of patients who had been healed during Kuhlman's church services. Casdorph studied their X-rays and laboratory films, personally discussed with the surgeons and physicians who treated them, asked qualified doctors to study the biopsy slides, brain scans and other medical data. In his book, *The Miracles*, Casdorph describes healings of ten terminal cases impossible to class as psychosomatic: cancers, rheumatoid and osteoarthritis, osteoporosis, multiple sclerosis and heart disease. These people were critically ill and most of them had been informed by their physicians that they were going to die.

One of them is Marion Burgio who was suffering from multiple sclerosis. Doctors have been diagnosing this ailment for two hundred years, but despite the immense volume of research and literature available, its mysteries still remain unsolved. Marion's problems begun in 1958 when she was twenty-nine years old. She first developed numbness in her hands and kept dropping the things she was trying to hold. She couldn't feel her legs anymore and when she tried to climb the stairs in her house she would fall on the floor. She tried to drive, but her car kept stalling. When her husband checked it, they discovered it wasn't the car, but in fact Marion couldn't feel her legs anymore and she wasn't pressing the gas pedal when she thought she was. She recalls taking things out of the oven without a pad or a glove, and the bath water was so hot it burned her skin but she wouldn't feel anything. She was too weak to even sit in a wheelchair.

In 1974, a friend insisted to take Marion to a Kathryn Kuhlman prayer meeting, but she refused to go arguing that she wants nothing to do with such things. Her friend pleaded with her and eventually Marion agreed to attend. On the morning of the service however, Marion woke up to the worst day of her life. Her body was trembling and shivering, her hand had twisted, and her eyes failed and she couldn't see. When her friend arrived to pick her up, Marion refused to go. They were watching TV together when suddenly both television sets in the house went out for no reason. Left without entertainment, Marion reluctantly got in the car and her friend drove to the prayer meeting. Once there, she was seated in the wheelchair section when the service begun. The choir sang praises to the Lord Jesus Christ when all of a sudden Marion found herself on her feet. Her hands straightened, the trembling in her body ceased and she could see and hear normally. She moved a few steps and to her wonder she realized that she could walk. After years of debilitating illness, she was healed on the spot. Marion later confessed she regarded Kuhlman to be a fraud and she attended the meeting only to please her friend who kept insisting she goes. "In this case there was marked deformity after twelve years of recurrent and persistent multiple sclerosis," noted Dr. Casdorph. "At the time of her healing, Marion was too weak to stand. She had lost control of her bowel and bladder and wore diapers, a humiliating experience for any cognizant adult. She had extremely poor vision plus double vision and marked hearing loss in her right ear. When Marion was literally raised from her chair during Kathryn Kuhlman's meeting at the Oakland Coliseum, all of these abnormalities instantly disappeared. The severely deformed left upper extremity sprung around in place like a rubber band."

Another case investigated by Dr. Casdorph was Marvin Bird who was diagnosed with arteriosclerotic heart disease, the most common cause of death in the United States. Marvin had his first heart attack when he was forty-six and then another two in the following years. When he turned sixty Marvin went for an angiography - a medical technique used to visualize the insides of blood vessels, arteries and heart chambers. His doctors - one of them being the medical expert examining the NASA astronauts before they flew into space, confirmed that his arteries were clogged and recommended Marvin to undergo a bypass surgery. He refused any medical intervention and left the hospital. Medication didn't help and his chest pains and heart condition got worse. Marvin became confined to bed, too weak to move and eventually quit eating. His family and friends expected him to die any day. His wife, Amy, insisted they attend a church service of Kathryn Kuhlman together and he agreed. During the meeting, one of Kuhlman's assistants asked Marvin to stand up and two ushers lifted him out of his wheelchair. He didn't feel anything, but discovered that he could stand by himself, which had been previously impossible. Instantly, his health and strength returned to his body. Marvin moved around for a while, but refused to testify on the platform about his healing because he didn't believe in miracles. When the prayer service ended, Marvin left his wheelchair in the auditorium and took his wife for a dinner in town. He hasn't had any chest pain and hasn't taken any medicine since. "When the medical professional confirmed that I was healed" recalled Marvin, "I really accepted the fact that a miracle happened to me. I just had to believe in God."

Some of the healing cases from Kathryn Kuhlman's services are notable for the wealth of medical data coming from prestigious universities and medical hospitals. One of them is Pearl Bryant who, at seventy-eight years old, was suffering from rheumatoid and osteoarthritis. She had been wearing leg braces for ten years and was forced to retire because she was having muscular spasms and blackouts while working with her students in the classroom. Pearl couldn't get into her car without somebody picking up her feet and putting them inside, a procedure that triggered excruciating pain. Doctors confirmed that there wasn't anything else they could do for her. "Bryant was pathetically crippled and plagued by excruciating pain," wrote Dr. Casdorph in his book. Pearl attended a Kathryn Kuhlman service and she was instantly healed. "I saw a vision of Jesus in a misty setting" she recalls. "He was smiling at me, He didn't speak, but His face assured me that everything was all right. He was wearing a white robe and He touched me on my shoulder and hand. His face impressed me the most. He was smiling."

The fact that a number of medical doctors and high-level professionals, including former U.S. Congressman and judge Samuel A. Weiss testify about Jesus Christ healing people, demonstrates that credible and intelligent people still witness His miracles even in our modern world today.

During another Kathryn Kuhlman service, Michael Harper, priest in the Church of England, was watching skeptically from the crowd. When Kuhlman spoke out that someone had been healed of emphysema and a young man begun running toward the auditorium, Harper was disgusted, suspecting a fraud. Irritated, Harper asked the man beside him what he thought of this scene, only to notice how deeply moved the man was. The man, it turned out, was the boy's father, who told Harper that until that evening the boy couldn't walk fifty yards without being out of breath. Doctors had told him that he would never run. "I learned a lesson that evening," repented Harper.

Kuhlman admitted that not everybody was healed and she attributed these miracles to God. She herself was never healed from an enlarged heart condition and accepted "medical treatment which she had often endorsed publicly as one of the means that God used to heal."

In 1970, *Time* magazine published an article about Kathryn Kuhlman in which they wrote that "miraculous cures seem to occur" at her services and named her "a veritable one-woman shrine of Lourdes." *Time* included four significant, medically attested cases of healing, including "a severely deteriorated eardrum" now with "no evidence of damage" and chronic lymphatic leukemia with swollen "liver, spleen and lymph nodes" now completely normal.

Kathryn Kuhlman traveled worldwide between the 1940s and 1970s holding church services, often reminding people that the healing of the body is not as important as the salvation of their soul. She often told audiences, "Jesus Christ knows you better than you know yourself. Today, He stands ready to hear your cry and to answer prayer for you. Look up and touch Jesus!"

2.

In times of long ago, a Nordic explorer set sails from his home in the Arctic lands and navigated across the ocean toward the Southern hemisphere. After months of voyage, the crew reached an island somewhere by the Equator. He disembarked on a sandy beach, saddled his horse and rode around to explore the territory. Under the tropical sun, the air was humid and hot year round. He reached a village where locals welcomed him with friendship in their homes. They shared a meal together and the explorer told them about life in the Arctic, how blizzards and snowstorms sweep across the land in winter and how even lakes freeze over for about a month.

"The frost had been so severe this winter" he said to them, "I rode my horse across a lake."

"That's impossible!" the villagers laughed. "This cannot be!"

"We have lakes here on our island and we have never seen anything like this" one of them said.

"It doesn't happen every day," replied the explorer. "Only sometimes during the winter months."

"Surely he must be lying," the locals grumbled among themselves.

"I am telling you the truth…Why don't you believe me?"

"What you are saying can't be true," one of them retorted. "We've never seen such things."

"It is impossible," said another and revolted. "Such matters do not exist!"

"Whether you believe me or not, I am telling you the truth," concluded the explorer. "The reality of this world is greater than what you currently know about it, that's all. If you are willing to believe my words, you will learn something new and your understanding of what is real will grow. But if you do not believe me, you do nothing but continue to live ignorant of a greater part of this reality. Nevertheless, what I have told you is true."

Dr. Joshua Brown, neuroscientist and professor at Indiana University, uses a simple mathematical model to explain how the human mind perceives and regards miracles. "The probability of accepting that an event has happened," Brown explains, "is equivalent to the prior assumption of the observer multiplied by the evidence of the event actually occurring. Basically, if your acceptance of the possibility for miracles is zero, then no matter how much evidence and data you are presented with, the probability for you to accept miracles as real is zero. Even if you see the data, because your acceptance of the possibility is zero, you will dismiss the evidence as forgery to maintain your belief." Simply stated, if you reject any possibility for miracles whatsoever, then God himself can come down from heaven and heal people before your very eyes and you will not believe. This mindset about miracles is similar to believing that the Earth is flat, but refusing to look at the photographs taken of the Earth from space to see the satellite images for yourself and realize that the Earth is round. Even if you do see these pictures of the Earth, you scrap them as fraud to maintain your belief. In reality, nobody by accepting or rejecting the possibility of miracles can change the reality of miracles being real, the Earth being round or lakes freezing in the Arctic during some winter months. If you give miracles zero chance to be authentic then you are not going to find any, but if you allow the possibility and look at the actual data with an open mind, you might be surprised at what you'll discover.

Dr. Craig Keener is an award-winning professor of New Testament and author of twenty-five academic books and more than 250 scientific articles. He is among the most respected and renowned Biblical scholars in the world. In the early 2000s, Keener spent a decade performing the largest scientific study in history on healing miracles done in the name of Jesus Christ. His academic book *Miracles - The Credibility of The New Testament Accounts* is a grand scholarly undertaking covering more than one thousand pages. Professors from prestigious universities around the world recognized his work as "the best book ever written on miracles in this or any age." Keener documented thousands of case studies from every continent on earth, with reports confirmed by eyewitnesses, testimonies validated by corroborating evidence and many examples backed by medical documentation. Even skeptics who investigated Keener's two volumes of miracles, while they didn't approve with all the case studies presented, in the end admitted they had found hundreds of accounts that can only be explained as miracles of God.

One of these cases is that of Bruce Van Natta. In 2006, Bruce was on duty in an auto service when the semitrailer truck he was working under collapsed and crushed him. His ribs were broken, the pancreas and spleen shattered and five major arteries severed. He was resuscitated and rushed to the hospital. Medical doctors gave Bruce him less than a year to live because he had lost 75 percent of his small intestine and couldn't eat anything. He went from 180 to 120 pounds and was withering away. One of his friends claimed that he felt led by God to fly from New York to Wisconsin to pray for Bruce. When he arrived in the hospital room, the man touched Bruce's forehead and said, "In the name of Jesus Christ, I command your intestine to grow!" Bruce recalls feeling an electric jolt going through his body and something coiling in his stomach. When the doctors examined Bruce, they discovered that the small intestine had doubled in length, which is medically impossible, and the pancreas and spleen had healed by themselves. History Channel produced a documentary about his case seeking to expose Bruce as a fraud, but when reporters investigated the medical documents they declared that this is a miracle. Studies at the University of Southern California also showed that nobody could have survived and recovered from the trauma that Bruce had suffered.

Another story reported by Keener is that of Ed Wilkinson, whose eight-year-old son Brad was found in 1984 to have atrial septal defect with two holes in his heart. The boy was already giving away his toys, not expecting to survive. One week before surgery, a minister asked Brad "Do you believe Jesus Christ can heal you?" to which he answered yes. The following Sunday the boy went in for surgery, but doctors discovered "there was nothing wrong with Brad's heart," although the two holes were clearly visible on the previous X-rays. "You can count this as a miracle," the surgeon told his father. The hospital risk manager also added, "You can see from the films, this was not a misdiagnosis."

Dr. Jacalyn Duffin, medical historian, President of the American Association for the History of Medicine and Canadian Society for the History of Medicine researched the vast archives of the Vatican and discovered more than 1,400 documented miracles from six continents dating from 1588 to 1999. The famous astronomer and cosmologist Carl Sagan once wrote that "it is far better to grasp the universe as it really is than to persist in delusion, however satisfying and reassuring." In the case of Jesus Christ still healing the sick today, "you cannot start with the premise that the uniform human experience excludes miracles, and then work from that premise by completely ignoring the witnesses and the evidence," concludes Dr. Keener.

3.

In 2004, The Jewish Theological Seminary performed a study in the United States across 1,087 physicians of diverse religious affiliations addressing the question, "Do doctors believe in miracles?" In the modern world, miracles seem antithetic to the scientific paradigm, but regardless of this prior belief, 74 percent of physicians believe miracles have occurred in the past and 73 percent believe miracles occur today. Surgeon Robert Orr, M.D. noted in an article in the Southern Medical Journal that, "a majority of physicians believe in miracles, though most agree that these are rare." One surprising discovery of the study was that more than half of the doctors

(55 percent) report having witnessed a medical miracle, 51 percent pray for their patients as a group and 60 percent pray for patients individually.

Medical doctors are among the most educated professionals in the world and earn an income that is generally among the top 5 percent of the population. A study performed by University of Chicago in 2005 showed that while the common belief is that science is contrary to faith, 76 percent of doctors in the United States believe in God. Dr. Rex Gardner M.D. is a well-credentialed physician who documented with medical evidence how people have healed from various debilitating illnesses after being praying for in the name of Jesus Christ. One of them is the case of a young medical trainee in North Wales who was dying of meningitis. X-ray films of her chest showed "extensive left-sided pneumonia with collapse of the middle lobe," but two days after she was prayed for, new X-rays showed a "normal chest." Gardner researched several cases, including a severe ulcer healed over night and a nine-year-old girl who was deaf but instantly healed to her audiologist's disbelief. The physician reported that "her hearing returned completely to normal. I can think of no rational explanation as to why her hearing returned to normal, while there being a severe sensorineural loss."

Dr. Cecil Titus of St. Luke's Hospital in Cleveland testifies that a ten-year old-girl's club foot "straightened before my very eyes while Miss [Kathryn] Kuhlman prayed." Dr. Kitman Au, a radiologist from California told a local newspaper, "I have seen healings in Kathryn Kuhlman's services that I, as a doctor, can only say go beyond human power." Dr. E.B. Henry reported his own instant healing of a false joint caused by a bone fracture and proved his claim with X-rays. Dr. Martin Biery, surgeon in a hospital in California recalls witnessing "arthritics whose spines were frozen get instantaneous freedom and move and bend in all directions without pain." Another Californian medical doctor, Viola Frymann testified to the healings she witnessed, including a blind child seeing and "another child, whose arm and leg were paralyzed from cerebral palsy healed before her eyes."A child almost blind from a blood clot on the optic nerve was instantly healed during one of Kathryn Kuhlman's services and the medical doctor testified that such a condition doesn't normally just vanish. Dr. James Blackann and Dr. Robert Hoyt attested the instant healing of a boy born with a deformed foot, who "walked up to the stage, ran back and forth, and skipped," after Kuhlman spoke from the platform that God was healing a child's legs. "I've seen massive cysts disperse immediately. I've seen spastic conditions disappear. I've seen arthritic spines and limbs instantly freed in her services," says Dr. Blackann. Dr. Keener tells the story of another medical doctor, John White, who certifies that a woman with a confirmed diagnosis of tuberculosis of the cervical spine was healed after prayer. "Her illness was certain, her cure permanent and the witness virtually incontrovertible." White was "bewildered to find there was no evidence of disease in her body." He later married the woman.

Dr. Charles Woodhouse, a board-certified orthopedic surgeon asked another trusted surgeon to pray for his daughter's epileptic seizures. After prayer, the seizures ceased. Teri Speed, M.D prayed for a man who was incurably blind due to a destroyed optic nerve and the man begun seeing that day. The same medical doctor prayed for a patient suffering from fibromyalgia and the illness went into immediate remission. Another university professor reported that two blind boys received sight and a deaf and mute was healed after prayer in Brazil. Professor Dan Montgomery prayed for a baby who had a whole in her heart and was scheduled for surgery the following week. "Not knowing what else to do, I put my hand on Julie's head and prayed my first ever prayer for physical healing," he recalls. The following week, the surgeon canceled the surgery showing her parents the X-rays confirming the hole had disappeared.

Dr. Chauncey Crandall, a world-class medical doctor prayed for a six-year-old boy who had never been able to walk and the boy begun running in front of tens of people. His parents fell to the ground weeping and the witnesses began shouting in joy. The same medical doctor reported seeing a disabled woman who was brought in a wheelbarrow to a prayer meeting in Mexico: "she got up on her feet and walked out!" Crandall also witnessed a deaf child instantly healed during prayer, a woman whose organs begun to shut down recovered, a flesh-eating ulcer healed in a few days, and two inoperable tumors disappeared after prayer documented with CT records.

Dr. Rex Gardner recalls the case of a blind schoolteacher whose sight was restored through prayer. His miracle was so complete that the man no longer needed the glasses he had worn for the previous twelve years. "Even in my limited survey," Dr. Keener noted," I have come across reports of more than 350 modern healings of blindness."

The reported cluster of miracles around the name of Jesus Christ is significant even in the Western medical communities. In 1995, Dee Sapp was rushed in and out of consciousness into the emergency room. Her body was so swollen from a cancer tumor in her colon that nurses initially believed that she was pregnant and took her to the delivery room. When the surgeon on duty, Dr. David Remedios read her medical data, he told her husband, "You don't have time to sign anything, you don't have time to do anything. If I don't operate on her immediately she is going to die." As Dee was being prepared for surgery, Remedios prayed "dear Jesus, your servant is in need of a miracle and undoubtedly you have chosen me and my hands to help you in this miracle today. I am asking you to allow the angels to show up in that operating room and I'm asking you to give me the gift of wisdom and the gift of knowledge to know what to do to your servant because she has to to have a miracle today." Remedios operated on Dee and took out three feet of her colon. He claimed that during surgery the Holy Spirit told him to stretch the remaining half of the colon, a procedure that has never been done before. This approach could have cost Remedios his medical license and Dee her life. He obeyed the insight and Dee made a full recovery. Most patients recover from this kind of surgery after four weeks, but Dee left the hospital in only a few days. Medical science confirms that colons do not grow back, but Dee later visited three different doctors and asked them "how many feet of colon do I have?" All of them confirmed she had six feet, as any normal person would have. What they didn't know was that three feet of colon had been previously removed, but miraculously grown back. "It doesn't matter where you are, what your circumstance is, there is nothing too difficult for God," says Dr. Remedios. Dee's miracle stood the test of time, as twenty-two years after her surgery she is healthy and travels the world sharing her testimony of God's healing power and mercy.

Sir John Polkinghorne is a former professor of mathematical physics at The University of Cambridge and laureate of the Templeton award. He writes: "science simply tells us that [miracles] are against normal expectation. We knew this at the start. Science cannot exclude the possibility that, on particular occasions, God does particular, unprecedented things. After all, God is the ordainer of the laws of nature, not someone who is subject to them." "That God does heal in the late twentieth century should be accepted on the evidence of all these case records" continues Dr. Rex Gardner. "If you do not accept those statements, you may ask yourself what evidence you would be prepared to accept. If the answer proves to be 'none,' then you had better face the fact that you have abandoned logical enquiry." Gardner concludes that "a belief in the occurrence of cases of miraculous healing today is intellectually acceptable." "Man prefers to believe what he prefers to be true," Francis Bacon once wrote, but upon completing his decade-long research into the miraculous healings in the name of Jesus Christ, Keener concluded that in the light of the overwhelming data available today "it is unscientific to deny miracles."

4.

Logan Knupp was only eight-months old when doctors diagnosed him with brain cancer. Surgeons removed a golf-sized tumor from his brain, but the following day MRI scans showed that the cancer metastasized and had spread throughout the entire length of his spinal cord. Doctors informed his parents to prepare for the worst, giving Logan only months to live. In the evening, hundreds of people gathered in the local church to pray for Logan. One elderly woman recalls having a vision during prayer with "the axe at the root of the cancer" and sensing God healing Logan. The following day doctors did another MRI scan and to their wonder found nothing. Dr. Jakacki, who treated Logan, says that this case is "a miracle with capital M." Another medical technician also confessed that "this is nothing short of a miracle." They ran several tests to verify the boy's condition at cellular level and concluded that Logan had been completely healed.

John Funderburg was only 32 years old when his heart failed. He was rushed to the intensive care unit where doctors informed his wife that John had very little chances to survive. His heart was operating at about 10 - 15 percent of its normal capacity and only a transplant could save his life. The church gathered in the evening to pray. Dr. Steven Hutchins, M.D., Medical Director of Baptist Health Transplant Institute, wrote a month later: "Mr. Funderburg came to the Baptist Medical Center with severe heart failure and in shock. He was gravely ill and being evaluated for heart transplantation at the time of his admission. I saw him in my office a month later and [without having a heart transplant], his repeat echo showed absolutely normal. Mr. Funderburg had a miraculous recovery."

Dr. Candy Gunther-Brown is a multiple award winning historian and ethnographer of culture and religion. She received her Ph.D. from Harvard University and is currently a Professor of religious studies at Indiana University. Her research is focused on investigating miracle claims around the world using the modern methods of science. In her scholarly book *Testing Prayer*, Dr. Brown notes the need for the testimonies of both medical doctors and patients to be considered as data, because medical documentation alone can never prove that a miracle has occurred even when documentation exists before and after prayer, nor can it demonstrate that God has actually healed the person. Even the most complete medical records can only show that doctors have previously diagnosed a patient with a disease or disability, no medical interventions have been performed or if they had been they failed to work, and then doctors can no longer detect physical evidence of the diagnosed problem and there is no natural medical explanation for how the healing occurred. Science cannot directly prove that the power of God has healed the person, but testimonies can connect the before with the after to provide insights into what took place.

On July 16, 1977, seven-year-old Ben Godwin was hit by a car while riding his bicycle. The accident splintered off three inches of his leg bone and doctors told him that if his leg was saved by surgery, he would limp for the rest of his life. Ben's mother continued praying and three months later X-rays showed that the entire bone had been restored, leaving physicians in awe. The bone graft operation was canceled. Godwin kept the X-rays for medical documentation.

Juan Santos was shot in the spine during World War II and remained paralyzed for sixteen years. He was instantly and permanently healed during prayer. The miracle is documented with official government records because Santos was a war veteran. (Stewart, Only Believe)

The Gospel of Mark documents Jesus instructing his early disciples: "These signs will follow those who believe…they shall lay hands on the sick and they shall recover." In 2016, a young woman from California was diagnosed with a rare neurological disease by which her own immune system was eating away her nervous system. She was fainting as much as forty-five times a day and couldn't walk anymore. Doctors at Stanford Medical Center gave her the devastating news that there was no cure for her illness. She started therapy trying to learn to walk again, but on January 2, 2017 she became crippled. On April 21 she cried out to God, telling Him that she cannot live this life anymore. The following morning as she was having breakfast with her husband in a cafe planning how to make it through this suffering, a little girl approached them. "I am learning to hear God's voice," the girl told them, "and I believe that God wants me to pray for you." The girl prayed, but nothing happened. Later, when the couple got back in the truck, both of her legs started convulsing uncontrollably. The husband drove to a park, where she got out and walked, and then ran for the first time in a year and a half. She recalls running and thinking within herself, "this is impossible, but it's happening." The husband filmed her healing and both cried tears of joy declaring how good God is.

Roxli Doss was only eleven years old when she was diagnosed with a terminal brain tumor by four different medical centers in Texas. Virginia Harrod, M.D. one of the girl's doctors declared that "we don't have a cure. This is considered a terminal diagnosis." Roxli's parents didn't have anyone to turn to but God. They prayed for a miracle and the entire community joined them in battle. On September 10, 2018, another MRI scan revealed the tumor had completely disappeared and Roxli was cancer free. Doctors didn't have any explanation for her healing. "When I first saw Roxli's MRI scan, it was actually unbelievable," Dr. Harrod recalls. "The tumor is undetectable on the MRI scan, which is really unusual." Even though her parents had been praying for a miracle, they themselves couldn't believe it when the miracle actually happened. "We all walked out in shock, even though we had been begging, praying, asking and believing. Thank you Jesus just wasn't enough to say."

On March 20, 1987, two-year-old Teresa Benedicta McCarthy swallowed sixteen times the lethal dose of Tylenol. Doctors at the Massachusetts General Hospital in Boston declared that Benedicta would die without a liver transplant. After a few days of prayer however, her liver and kidneys fully recovered without a transplant. Her main physician, Dr. Ronald Kleinman, associate professor of pediatrics at Harvard Medical School considered her healing miraculous and reported it to the Vatican and to the American media.

Robert DeGrandis documented numerous miracle accounts including the complete healing after prayer of a five-year-old girl whose ribs were broken and her spleen ruptured in an accident, and of another child disabled and fed intravenously for fourteen years who was completely healed after Jesus Christ appeared to her in a vision.

Dr. David C. Lewis, social anthropologist and lecturer at the University of Cambridge investigated the healing claims in the ministry of John Wimber and found that roughly one-third of those prayed for received healing. Cases include healings of hernia, sensitive teeth, hip pain, hip injury, spine injury and injuries resulting from car crashes.

One of the most systematic initiatives to document miracle healings in the twenty-first century with clear-cut medical data is the World Christian Doctors Network (WCDN) founded in 2004 by a group of Christian doctors from Korea. The organization documents miracle healings in hospitals and collects patient histories and diagnoses illustrated by medical evidence, X-rays, computer tomography, endoscopic, microscopic and other data recorded using the latest medical technologies. WCDN has a database of miracle cases documented in detail, including healings of metastasized cancers, heart attacks, sterility, pulmonary tuberculosis, herniated discs, intra-cerebral bleeding, hearing loss, blindness, severe skin burns, ebola and tuberculosis. "Miracles are not contrary to nature," Saint Augustine wrote in the ancient past, "but only to what we know about nature." WCDN has built a database of miracle healings performed in the name of Jesus Christ to expand our knowledge and understanding of nature and of Him who has power over it.

5.

The Bible documents Jesus Christ telling people, "Go back and report to John what you have seen and heard: the blind receive sight, the lame walk, those who have leprosy are cleansed, the deaf hear, the dead are raised." Since the days when Jesus walked the shores of Galilee until today, those who have been miraculously healed are transformed by the experience. Skeptics might discard their claims, but nothing can take their miracle away. Those who had been healed through prayer become in turn messengers of God's love to people. "The effects of a single healing experience reverberate across a global network, as recipients become aware of a new possibility, turn their attention to others and join the efforts of spreading God's love to humanity," noted Dr. Candy Gunther-Brown. Every person who is healed through prayer in the name of Jesus Christ immediately goes out and tells others what God has done for them.

Dr. Ramsay MacMullen, emeritus professor of history at Yale University, discovered in his research that the leading cause of conversions from polytheism to Christianity in the third and forth centuries was miraculous healings. Dr. J.P. Moreland, distinguished professor of theology at Biola University, found that roughly 70 percent of the conversions to Christianity in history took place as a result of miracles. In recent years, 50 percent of conversions to Christianity in China happened because of miraculous healings. Researchers found that "according to some surveys, 90 percent of new believers in China cite healing as a reason for their conversion." Craig Keener also noted that millions of people are leaving their ancient traditions and the cultural beliefs held for generations to follow Jesus Christ as a result of miracle healings.

Danyun tells the story of a blind boy from China who was very ill. His father asked some Christian ministers to pray for him, but they doubted and urged him to turn to directly to God.

The man "removed the idols from his home to declare his faith in God" and "his son immediately showed signs of improvement." Two days later the doctor declared the boy healed and "after three days he received his sight." Many people in the region turned to follow Jesus Christ because of this miracle, though ministers were ashamed for their lack of faith.

People in the Western world also believe miracles are real. A Gallup poll showed in 1989 that 82 percent of the people in the United States believe in miracles. A 1996 poll suggests that around 80 percent of patients believe that prayer can be helpful in their healing. Seventy-two percent of the U.S. respondents in a 2003 Newsweek poll believe that God may heal even a mortally ill person on whom doctors had given up. A Pew Forum survey concluded that 79 percent believe that "miracles still occur today as in ancient times." Another 2006 research study performed in ten countries estimated that around 200 million people claimed to have experienced or witnessed miracles. Lee Strobel, former atheist turned Christian evangelist commissioned a research study that showed that 94 million adults in America would say they've had an experience they can only explain as a miracle from God. "Globally, based on surveys, this number is in the hundreds of millions," writes Strobel. A poll by USA Today, ABC News and Stanford University Medical Center found that more than half of respondents used prayer for healing. Of those who prayed, 90 percent found it effective and 51 percent highly effective. Another study in Brazil asked people if they had ever received divine healing of an illness or disability and 59 percent reported experiences of God healing them. The great majority of them - 80 percent, were physical healings, rather than mental or emotional problems.

On July 20, 2008 eleven-year-old Kayla Knight was diagnosed with a tumor that covered nearly a forth of her brain. Two days after prayer and before any medical treatment could begin, another MRI showed that the tumor was gone. The healing was confirmed with an ulterior MRI scan.

Dr. Candy Gunther-Brown recalls the case of Sylvia, a Brazilian singer whom the doctors had sent home to die from cancer of thorax. In 2005, Sylvia went to a prayer meeting a mere eighty pounds. She was too weak to stand and was coughing up blood. Evangelist Randy Clark and his team spent one hour praying for Sylvia and she claimed feeling the power and love of God going through her body. After prayer, Sylvia felt strong enough to stand up and sing a song of praise to God. She was healed and two years later, Sylvia was still symptom-free. She regained a healthy weight and returned to her job.

In 1999, sociologist Margaret Poloma and political scientist John Green studied healing experiences among Christians. They surveyed 1,827 people from twenty-one church congregations in the United States and found that 70 percent have experienced a miraculous healing from a physical illness, 85 percent had "witnessed a miraculous healing in the lives of family members and friends," and 93 percent had personally had "an emotional healing."
One of the cases documented is of a woman addicted to cigarettes for twelve years. "I smoked from the age of eleven," she testified. "I became a Christian when I was twenty-three years old. I had tried for years to quit - I had even smoked through pregnancies, but I couldn't. Two weeks after I got saved, they had an altar call for people to be delivered of a habit. I didn't think to go, but my sister nudged me, so I went. The pastor prayed for me, he laid hands on me and commanded the spirit of nicotine to come out. I was not familiar with these terms, but I left the church that night not having any desire to smoke. It's now been 25 years and I have never had the desire [to smoke again], not even once." Another man confessed, "after being saved, God delivered me from 25 years of alcohol addiction."

In the 1900s, theologian Dietrich Bonhoeffer wrote that "truth divorced from experience must always dwell in the realm of doubt," or in other words doubts will arise in the minds of those who haven't experienced a miracle. However, as professor Danny McCain noted, "it is arrogant and unprofessional for [some] Western scholars to outright reject the miraculous, totally ignoring the testimonies of thousands of people" simply based on their lack of such experience. Many of the best scholars recognize today that "healing testimonials claiming recovery from every condition from headaches to cancers are too numerous to count," and that healing is cited in many instances as the primary motivator for following Jesus Christ.

6.

The Book of Psalms declares that God "forgives all my sins and heals all my diseases." God "heals the brokenhearted and binds up their wounds." Whenever people cried to God for help in times of trouble, "He saved them from their distress. He sent out his word and healed them, snatching them from the door of death." Somebody once warned, "be careful how you listen to what you hear. Measure everything against what Jesus Christ has spoken. If you open your mouth and speak against his words, although unwillingly, you make yourself greater than Christ and more knowledgable than him. If Jesus instructed that in his name you will heal the sick, raise the dead and do far greater things, but yet you say this simply is not true, then you are saying you know better. If you don't understand his words, seek wisdom and pray for revelation, but if you reject his words without knowing any better and claim the opposite is true, you render Christ a liar, a madman or a fool." Medical data, however, confirms his every word.

In 1987, Charles Ndifon was a high-school student in Nigeria. On a Sunday just like any other, at 3 o'clock in the afternoon Jesus Christ appeared to him. His first thought was "I'm so unclean. Lord. If I've done anything wrong, I repent of everything I've ever done" recalls Charles. "I thought I was dead. Jesus looked straight at me and never condemned me. His eyes were full of liquid love. All Jesus said was "Go and preach the gospel. As I was with those in the past, so I will be with you. If people can believe the message you give them, no sickness and no disease will stand against you." After this encounter "I knew that Jesus was alive," says Ndifon. He has since traveled to eighty seven countries preaching the gospel, healing the sick, telling people "Jesus is alive. Had he not been alive, Jesus wouldn't do all these miracles. The miracles themselves are the proof that he is alive." Charles Ndifon documents on film his services and keeps in Rhode Island an archive of miracles captured on camera in the past twenty years.

Henriette was only a young woman, but she had been crippled by multiple sclerosis. She was in a wheelchair, and in six years the illness had brought her to the point where she needed four or five caregivers a day to tend to her basic needs. Her mother decided to take her by force to Ndifon's meetings in Denmark. Henriette didn't believe in any of "those hallelujah meetings," and although she witnessed several people walking out of their wheelchairs, she thought they had been planted to pretend they were sick and had been healed. When Ndifon's team prayed for her, "something like an electric shock ran through me and I burst into tears," she recalls. Henriette dropped the crutches and begun walking by herself. She was instantly healed. The following day she went for a long walk with her mother, played football with her friends and climbed trees with her nephew. "God created everything," says Ndifon, "and He should be able to regenerate an eye or an ear drum, to get the nerves to function again and the feet to walk again."

Henri Nissen is one of the Danish journalists who attended the healing services of Dr. Charles Ndifon in year 2000. In his book *The God of Miracles*, Nissen documented tens of miracle accounts from Ndifon's ministry. These miracles have been recorded on film, documented with medical data and hospital records, and some have even been featured on national television.

The Danish media planted Roger in the audience in one of Ndifon's meetings to show to the public that "this preacher is a fraud" and that people who claimed to have been healed have been paid and planted for the show. Roger had an accident that resulted in a skull fracture, one eye had lowered and he developed a chronic impairment known as double vision. For three months after the incident Roger had shut himself in the house depressed as his life turned unbearable. During the meeting, Ndifon asked people in the audience if they wanted to believe in Jesus Christ. Roger looked around not knowing what to do and eventually raised his hand. Ndifon laid his hands on him and asked Roger to remove his eyepatch. To his wonder, he could see perfectly clear. He had been healed on the spot. The television crew who planted Roger didn't even notice his healing, but later found Roger in the hall of the building. One of the colleagues who put him in the audience said, "the whole team stood with tears in our eyes. It was simply impossible to maintain professional distance when something like this happened." The journalists also learned that Charles Ndifon didn't claim to have any healing powers or magical abilities. "I am not a miracle worker or healer," he repeatedly says. "I am just a messenger from God who talks about what Jesus Christ can do for people." Medical doctors confirmed Roger's healing at the Danish

National Hospital. "The secret to healing," instructs Ndifon, "is to take your eyes off your sickness and keep your eyes on Jesus. You become what you look upon. Behold Jesus and live."

Kristian was one of the thousands of people who attended Charles Ndifon's meeting in Denmark. He was only a young man, but he had been crippled for ten years as the result of a knee injury and was suffering from cruciate ligament ruptures and degenerative arthritis. "I had trouble believing that a short prayer could sort out what the doctors had not been able to do," Kristian confessed. Ndifon prayed for him and "a powerful heat spread throughout my body, the heat rushed down to my knee where it gathered," recalls Kristian. He then threw away the crutches and started walking. He was instantly healed. The miracle was captured by the media and featured on national television. Ndifon tells people that "God's word is His medicine" and we should take His word (The Bible) at face value and believe it. Words are seeds and the words of Jesus Christ are filled with God's power and bring healing when they are believed."

However, "many want the healing, but not the healer," noticed Ndifon. "Jesus Christ is the healer, and in order for you to be healed, Jesus has to live in you." When you surrender your life to Christ and he reigns in you, his life invades your being. His power drives out everything that is not of God. His Spirit throws out illness, fear, anxiety, depression, shame, unworthiness and guilt. When Jesus reigns in you, you literally begin life once more. Jesus Christ must rule in your life in truth, not in your head, in ideas, philosophies or religion. If Jesus is your very life, you will have life. But if Jesus is just an idea, you will have nothing. "Truth changes your life when you have a revelation of it," says Ndifon. When you open the doors for Christ to live in you, sometimes the healing is immediate and sometimes it takes a bit of time. Jesus never promised instant healing, but he promised that "all things are possible for those who believe."

After another meeting Ndifon held in Denmark with more than eighteen hundred participants, about four hundred wrote letters to the local church testifying they had been healed during service. A lady from Iran who was initially convinced that the prayer meeting was a fraud and "those healed were just actors paid to pretend" was instantly healed herself of a slipped disc after suffering terrible pain for ten years. Henri Nissen documented healing cases of back pains, whiplash, polio, epilepsy, terminal cancers, heart problems, blindness, deafness, infertility, rheumatoid arthritis, osteoporosis and others.

In 2000, Charles Ndifon visited the Goa University Medical Center in India. The children in the intensive care unit were suffering with terminal diseases, including AIDS, cancers and diabetes, and some were in a coma about to die. Forty children were discharged in a day or two after they had been prayed for. These miracles have been documented in hospital records and parents provided photographs with the empty beds in the intensive care ward. A little boy who drank kerosene was unconscious in a coma, but after Ndifon prayed for him he revived and left the hospital. In one of Ndifon's crusades in Zimbabwe, a man paralyzed for 10 years and confined to a wheel chair stood up in front of thousands of people and walked. In Mexico, a woman was carried by her family on a stretcher to Ndifon's church service. Her lungs had been removed and doctors had given up on her. She had been confined to bed for years, breathing through an oxygen tank and waiting for death to take her. Ndifon told her that nothing is impossible with God if she can only believe. He commanded new lungs to be formed in her. She then removed her oxygen tank and immediately begun breathing by herself. She stood up from the stretcher and slowly started walking. These miracles were filmed and archived at Christ Love Ministries.

One of the main reasons many are not healed is because religious people and traditional churches have taught for years that we shouldn't expect God to intervene in our lives. These people honor their own beliefs, but dishonor God with their very words. Jesus said "these signs will accompany those who believe: in my name they will lay their hands on the sick and they will recover." If religious people teach opposite to Jesus Christ, they dishonor him with their very teaching. In the modern world, God always comes last and this if He hasn't been completely forgotten. We trust ourselves, rely on other people and run to all the experts before we come to God and cry for help. When doctors give up, when there is nothing left for them to do and our world comes crumbling down, only then we turn to God, wondering if He is real and doubting if He wants to heal us. In a university lecture, Craig Keener posed the question: According to the data, "Jesus performs miracles today. Why then doubt the words of the gospels?" Come to Jesus, because He is alive. The One who gave you life, is alive. The One who gave you eyes, sees you. The One who gave you ears and tears hears your prayers and your cry for help. If Jesus wasn't alive, he wouldn't do these miracles to confirm his words. Anything is possible, if you can only believe.

CHAPTER 3
One More Chance

Q3 - Does Jesus raise the dead today?

"Which is harder, to be born or to rise again? That what has never been should be, or that what has been should be once more?" - Blaise Pascal

1.

On Friday, November 30, 2001, Daniel Ekechukwu was driving his twenty-year old Mercedes Benz to his's father's village in Nigeria. Going down a hill, Daniel hit the brake several times, but the pedal went straight to the floor and his car crashed into a concrete pillar. Daniel's chest and head smashed into the steering wheel. He was rushed to the nearest medical clinic, his pregnant wife Nneka joining him in the ambulance. On the way, Daniel started having difficulties breathing, he told her he loved her, closed his eyes and breathed his last.

When they arrived at the medical center, Dr. Jose Annebunwa examined the body and informed the family that they had arrived too late. Daniel had no breathing, no pulse, no heartbeat. "It was as if life went out of me," his wife recalls, "I was shouting." The doctor signed off the death certificate and requested his colleagues to take Daniel to the mortuary.

Later that evening, his friends transported Daniel's body to the village where his family was living and put him in the funeral home. The local mortician verified his body one more time, also confirming that Daniel was dead, and scheduled him for embalming.

The following day, Saturday, family members came at his father's house to mourn for Daniel. Nneka lamented and cried, "I begun to call upon the name of the Lord. I begun to remind God of his promises. In *[The Book of] Isaiah*, the Lord says that I shall not experience violence in my home again. This is one of the violences that has come and You promised me that I would not experience them again. Why this one?" she cried out to God. "Another Bible verse that inspired me was [from The Epistle to the] Hebrews," Nneka continued, "women received back their dead, raised to life again." No, this cannot happen. I must do something to prove God," she cried. The funeral had been scheduled, but Nneka pleaded with Daniel's father not to bury him, but instead to take him to a prayer meeting at their church on Sunday. His father agreed, but the following morning when they went to the funeral home, Daniel's body had already been embalmed, cotton stuffed in his nostrils, and placed in the coffin.

Some friends took Daniel with the coffin, placed him in the back of an ambulance, and drove to the local church where evangelist Reinhard Bonnke was preaching. Nneka insisted to bring Daniel inside the church hall where thousands of people were attending service, but the security guards refused to let the family bring the dead body inside, reasoning with her that it would frighten the people. "I believe he is going to come back to life!" she shouted and refused to leave. Eventually, one of the pastors agreed to let them stay, but took Daniel's body to the basement of the building where they removed him from the coffin and laid him on a table.

In the auditorium, unaware of what was happening outside, Bonnke finished preaching and concluded the meeting with a prayer for the people in the audience. He then went into the office, when somebody thrust the door open and cried out, "He's breathing! He's breathing!"

Daniel's chest begun moving up and down. "Although he is breathing," his father noticed, "his body is still like iron." Two pastors who were with him in the basement begun praying and they recalled observing how life was coming back into his body. His eyes then started moving and his heart begun to beat. Somebody ran upstairs and broke the news, and a crowd of people rushed into the basement to see what was taking place. All of a sudden, upon hearing the crowd screaming and shouting, Daniel jumped up on the table. He turned his head and gazed at the commotion happening around him. The pastors then took Daniel upstairs in the auditorium and sat him in a chair where he completely recovered. His story, the medical data, the eyewitness testimonies and the event itself of Daniel coming back to life was captured on camera and documented in Reinhard's Bonnke's film *Raised from the Dead*. The following day, Monday, Daniel visited the pastor of the local church. "He was still smelling of embalming chemicals," the pastor recalled. Daniel told everyone how he had seen heaven and hell before he was given one last chance to testify to people and urge them to return to God by believing in Jesus Christ.

2.

The books of the New Testament record the first apostles of Jesus Christ posing a simple question to the crowds: "Why should any of you consider it incredible that God raises the dead?"

The gospels document Jesus bringing back several people from the dead. On one account, "messengers arrived from the home of Jairus, the leader of the synagogue. They told him, "Your daughter is dead. There's no use troubling [Jesus] now." But Jesus overheard them and said to Jairus, "Don't be afraid. Just have faith." Then Jesus stopped the crowd and wouldn't let anyone go with him except Peter, James and John. When they came to the home of the synagogue leader, Jesus saw much commotion and weeping and wailing. He went inside and asked, "Why all this commotion and weeping? The child isn't dead, she's only asleep." The crowd laughed at him. But he made them all leave, and he took the girl's father and mother and his three disciples into the room where the girl was lying. Holding her hand, he said to her, "Little girl, get up!" And the girl, who was twelve years old, immediately stood up and walked around! They were overwhelmed and totally amazed. Jesus gave them strict orders not to tell anyone what had happened, and then he told them to give her something to eat." (*The Gospel of Luke*)

On another occasion, "[Jesus] went to a town called Nain, and his disciples and a great crowd went with him. As he drew near to the gate of the town, a man who had died was being carried out, the only son of his mother, and she was a widow, and a considerable crowd from the town was with her. And when the Lord saw her, he had compassion on her and said to her, "Do not weep." Then he came up and touched the bier, and the bearers stood still. And he said, "Young man, I say to you, arise." And the dead man sat up and began to speak, and Jesus gave him to his mother. Fear seized them all and they glorified God." (*The Gospel of Luke*)

The Gospel of John records Jesus raising a man named Lazarus after being in the grave for four days. On that day, Jesus "arrived at the tomb, a cave with a stone rolled across its entrance. "Roll the stone aside," he told them. But Martha, the dead man's sister, protested, "Lord, he has been dead for four days. The smell will be terrible." Jesus responded, "Didn't I tell you that you would see God's glory if you believe?" So they rolled the stone aside. Then Jesus looked up to heaven and said, "Father, thank you for hearing me. You always hear me, but I said it out loud for the sake of all these people standing here, so that they will believe You sent me." Then Jesus shouted, "Lazarus, come out!" And the dead man came out, his hands and feet bound in grave clothes, his face wrapped in a head cloth. Jesus told them, "Unwrap him and let him go!"

Not only Jesus raised the dead, but some of his early followers also brought people back from beyond the grave. *The Book of Acts* recalls the following account: "A woman who was a follower [of Jesus] lived in the city of Joppa. Her name was Tabitha (or Dorcas in Greek). She did many good things and many acts of kindness. One day she became sick and died. After they had washed her body, they laid her in a room on the second floor. The city of Lydda was near Joppa. The followers heard that Peter was at Lydda and sent two men to ask him to come at once. Peter went back with them. When he came, they took him to the room. All the women whose husbands had died were standing around crying. They were showing the clothes Dorcas had made while she was with them. Peter made them all leave the room. Then he got down on his knees and prayed. He turned to her body and said, "Tabitha, get up!" She opened her eyes and looked at Peter and sat up. He took her by the hand and lifted her up. Then he called in the faithful followers and the women whose husbands had died. He gave her to them, a living person."

The Bible describes Jesus Christ and his early disciples raising the dead. Skeptics dismiss the accounts of the New Testament as nothing but religious myths. Therefore, looking through the lens of modern science, the question is - does Jesus and his followers still raise the dead today?

3.

On October 20, 2006, Jeffrey Markin walked into Palm Beach Gardens Hospital in Florida and collapsed from a severe heart attack. The medical team rushed Jeffrey into the emergency room, but forty five minutes later he was pronounced dead. The supervising cardiologist, Dr. Chauncey Crandall, filled out the report. He recalls Markin was unusually obviously dead - his face, fingers and toes had already turned black. When this happens, there is little hope to revive a patient. Crandall finalized the papers and started walking towards the door. "Before I crossed the threshold," he recalls, "I sensed God telling me to turn around and pray for the patient." He returned, and in front of his colleagues, Crandall prayed for Jeffrey to have a second chance at life. "Father God, I cry out for the soul of this man. If he doesn't know you as his Lord and Savior, please raise him from the dead right now, in Jesus's name." Crandall then requested his team to give the man another shock with the defibrillator. Instantly, Jeffrey returned to life. Soon thereafter he was completely healed. Asked if the man couldn't have revived from the final shock, Crandall confirmed that "the team tried to revive him for 45 minutes using the standard American Heart Association protocols and this resuscitation could not have happened naturally."

On October 24, 2008, Dr. Shawn George, a medical doctor from Australia suffered a heart attacked and was rushed to the hospital. The medical team worked on Shawn for one hour and ten minutes, and gave him thirteen electrical shocks with a defibrillator and over 4,000 cardiac compressions. When blood supply to the brain is interrupted for 3 minutes, the brain cells begin to die and after 20 minutes the organ is completely dead. This is the reason why cardiopulmonary resuscitation (CPR) is rarely performed for more than 30 minutes. In Shawn's case, doctors had stopped all life support measures except oxygen to the lungs and pronounced him dead. The senior physician then called his wife to say goodbye. She walked into the emergency room where Shawn's body was lying on the table, took his hand and said a simple prayer: "Lord Jesus, Shawn is only 39, I am only 38, we have a ten-year-old boy. I need a miracle." Suddenly his heart started beating with a weak pulse. He had been dead for one hour and twenty five minutes. His colleagues rushed in, operated on him although very doubtful that he will survive. However, Shawn made a complete recovery and three months later he was back to work. Reading his own medical charts, he says "there aren't many well documented cases of patients being clinically dead for so long, returning to life with their memory perfectly intact and without any neurological problems at all. Medically, this is impossible. It could only be done by God."

On January 19, 2015, fourteen-year-old John Smith fell through the ice into the frozen Lake St. Louise is St. Charles, Missouri. The eight-grader was walking on the ice-covered lake with two friends when the ice suddenly broke. He fell through and sank to the bottom of the lake. By the time paramedics found him, John had been submerged for more than a quarter of an hour. The emergency crew attempted CPR for 15 minutes and medical doctors at SSM St. Joseph Hospital West continued procedures for another 27 minutes. "He was gone," declared Dr. Nancy Bauer, pediatrician. "I've never felt someone so cold in my life." John didn't have a heartbeat and any vital signs for 45 minutes. He was dead. Then, John's mother Joyce, came into the hospital room and cried out to Jesus, "please send your Holy Spirit to save my son, please save him!" Instantly his heart started beating. "His mother came in the room, yelled out "Come Holy Spirit!" and "a few seconds later, we had a heartbeat," recalls Dr. Bauer. "It gave me goosebumps." Nurse Wendy Hoff who was also present in room declared with tears in her eyes that "it was a miracle. Everybody just started crying." "He was dead for 45 minutes," recalls Dr. Kent Sutterer, the principal physician on the case, and then "within a matter of a minute or two, his heart started again." The next morning John opened his eyes and in a few weeks made a complete recovery. Dr. Jeremy Garrett, one of the experts who treated the boy, confessed that his recovery remains like nothing he had ever seen and "it is a bonafide miracle." John's dad commented that what happened to John might seem unbelievable to our modern skeptical world, but regardless of that, "you cannot refute the clinical evidence." Medical doctors wrote in a letter, "the heart was jumpstarted by the Holy Spirit listening to the request of his praying mother."

William Standish Reed, M.D. (1922-2010) graduated from the University of Michigan's Medical School as Valedictorian and later received his Master of Science in Surgery. He served in the U.S. Navy as a medical officer and worked as a surgeon in the U.S. and abroad. Reed reports the cases of two children apparently dead (one of them being his own) who returned to life through prayer in the name of Jesus Christ.

In 1992 in China, Zhao Yu-e was pronounced dead upon arriving at the hospital at 10 o'clock in the morning. Despite mockery and public ridicule, some people prayed for her and the next morning Zhao returned to life. The hospital superintendent immediately inquired how he can become a follower of Jesus Christ.

If respiration has ceased for six minutes, brain damage is normally irreversible even if the person is revived using modern medical technology. Most of the contemporary accounts of people raised from the dead involve longer periods of time, yet those revived lack signs of brain damage, therefore defying medical expectations.

One example is one-year-old John Eric Cadenhead who had no vital signs for 40 minutes. After prayer, he was restored with no brain damage. The staff at Huntington Hospital documented his recovery in 1982 and regarded it as miraculous.

On January 18, 1989, Don Piper was killed in a car wreck in Texas. He was pronounced dead by the first paramedic on the scene and by other three emergency medical technicians. His body lay under a tarp for 90 minutes. A pastor who drove by the scene asked rescuers for the permission to pray for the victim, and after a few minutes of prayer Don's heart started beating again. His physical recovery was difficult and took a long time, but nonetheless Don returned to life and testified about visiting heaven and encountering dead relatives.

Dr. J. Ayodeji Adewuya is a professor of New Testament in the United States. On January 1, 1981, his newborn baby was pronounced dead at birth. After twenty minutes of prayer he returned to life, his father witnessing the event. The boy grew up to be a healthy man.

Professor Michael J. McClymond describes the case of Elouise Jordan from Memphis, Tennessee. In 1940, at thirty-three years old, Elouise was diagnosed with cancer in the throat. She was admitted at John Gaston Hospital, but doctors sent her home because there was nothing else they could do. She fought the illness for nine years but the cancer ate her throat and destroyed her ability to speak. In 1949, her daughter Katherine was called home because Eloise had died. A funeral hearse from J.O. Patterson mortuary already arrived in front of the house. Before they could take her however, local bishop Charles Mason "prayed and rebuked death, and life came back into Elouise's body." When Katherine reached home, her mother "was on the porch in a pink night gown, dancing and praising God." Eloise's speech capability also returned. She died of natural causes 33 years later.

In 1985, evangelist Mahesh Chavda was on the platform speaking to thirty thousand people in a town in Congo, when he claimed that the Spirit of God told him: "There is a man here whose son died this morning. Call him to come forward. I want to do something wonderful for him." Chavda repeated these words in the microphone and a man ran to the front of the crowd. They prayed for the resurrection of his son, then the man ran off back through the multitudes. Chavda learned only later what had occurred. The man's name was Manikai Mulamba and his six-year-old son had died eight hours before of cerebral malaria. Doctors pronounced the child dead and signed off the death certificate, but because the father couldn't afford the burial permit, he left the boy in the hospital trying to find some money. Manikai's brother stayed to watch over the lifeless body of the child. Manikai, who was one of the few people in his family who was a Christian, prayed to Jesus Christ: "I have told many people that you are the Good Shepherd. How will they believe me if my own son dies?" Running through the streets of his town, Manikai claimed that he heard the Spirit of God telling him, "Why are you weeping? My servant is in the city. Go to him." Manikai ran through the crowd where Chavda was speaking and just as he arrived he heard Chavda call forth the man whose son had died. He went to the platform, Chavda prayed for his son and Manikai rushed back to the hospital. His brother then continues the story. "It was midday. I was sitting there holding the body of my brother's son in my arms. Suddenly, I felt his body move. He sat up in my arms and asked for something to eat." Chavda provided documentation for the miracle.

Andrew White, priest in the only Anglican church in Iraq and also known as the "Vicar of Baghdad," recalls the story of a Muslim man who's wife was dying in the hospital. The man came to White and begged him to come and pray for his wife in the name of his god. White couldn't leave his work to go to the hospital, but instructed him to pray by calling on Jesus Christ. The man rushed back to the hospital, but when he arrived the doctors told him that his wife had already died. In despair, he went into the ward, hugged his wife's body and lamented over her saying "Jesus! Jesus! Jesus…!" Suddenly she gasped for air and told him "I'm hungry."

Prayer in the name of Jesus Christ is the common element in these accounts from all over the world. Many people have abandoned their ancient beliefs to follow Jesus, sometimes with the cost of persecution, indicating that something extraordinary had taken place in their life.

Dr. Julie Ma tells the story of a woman from Nepal. Although prayers and sacrifices had been made to local deities, Tamang's mother died. For several hours, a Buddhist lama chanted prayers over her, but she remained dead. Willing to try anything, her son brought some Christians from a neighboring village to pray for her. They prayed and "his mother came back to life" in front of the entire village who had gathered to see what was happening. More than 160 people left their ancestral traditions and became followers of Jesus Christ that day.

In India, a high government official's son was close to death. The family offered sacrifices to local deities, but the boy died. Finding that his son had passed away several hours earlier, his father took the advise of a pharmacist who suggested he should try and pray to the God of the Christians, Jesus. The father promised Jesus to worship him if he brought his son back to life.

"Immediately, the eyes of the child began to flicker again and he was restored to life." Hundreds of people in the region committed themselves to Jesus Christ.

"While obviously the vast majority of people who die are not raised, the pattern of so many being raised in conjunction to prayer to Jesus Christ suggests more than coincidence, all the more so when these persons have been dead too long to be resuscitated naturally," comments Dr. Craig Keener. He often presents in his university lectures the case of a boy from India who was found dead at the bottom of a swimming pool. He was rushed to the hospital, where doctors pronounced him dead. Ninety minutes later he opened his eyes and testified that he heard the name Jesus, and then life returned to his body. His parents confirmed that the boy had never heard this name before. In his academic book *Miracles,* Keener presents numerous raising accounts from every corner of the earth. He collected eye-witness testimonies of people being raised from the dead in the name of Jesus Christ from credible sources, including medical doctors, scholars, professionals, and even his own family members. After a decade-long investigation, Keener reached the conclusion that "raising claims are in fact numerous today." William P. Wilson, professor emeritus of psychiatry at Duke University Medical Center also notes regarding miracles that "in spite of protestations by some scientists, documented events occur regularly both in this country (United States) and in the rest of the world."

Many contemporary miracle accounts are similar in kind to those reported about Jesus Christ and his early followers. The gospels document only a small number of people raised from the dead compared to the masses who heard Jesus's message. It is important to understand that just as only few have been raised from the dead by Jesus and his first apostles, only some are revived today through prayer in his name. Nonetheless, the growing body of medical evidence and eyewitness testimonies confirm the fact that Jesus Christ still raises the dead today.

CHAPTER 4
The Seed

Q4 - Does Jesus cast out demons today?

"If it can be destroyed by the truth,
it deserves to be destroyed by the truth" - Carl Sagan

1.

Brian opened the door and invited me into his living room where we sat down in two leather armchairs facing each other. His wife brought tea and cookies, and put the tray on the table besides an old worn-out Bible with leather covers and bookmarks of all colors coming out it. Before I stepped inside, I pictured Brian's house with crucifixes and scripture quotes on the walls, but there weren't any. The living room was painted in a warm beige and only several black and white photographs with him dressed in military uniform flying in warplanes were hanging on the walls.

"I was a jet fighter pilot in the U.K. Royal Air Force" said Brian as he passed me the cup of tea.

"How did you go from flying military planes to being a minister for Jesus Christ?" I asked.

"Back in the 70s, the Irish Republican Army, also known as IRA, was a terrorist group fighting to unite the Northern counties of Ireland with the rest of the country. Most people, however, didn't want reunification with Ireland and this terrorist band detonated bombs in public places, murdered civilians and shed innocent blood. The Royal Air Force had been deployed to maintain peace in Northern Ireland, and in 1973 they sent me there for the third time in a row. I was the commanding officer of my platoon, responsible for protecting the City of Londonderry. Or

Derry, as locals call it. We were on duty twelve to fourteen hours a day in all weathers, verifying vehicles for bombs, searching pedestrians for guns, looking for weapons and explosives, whist all the time watching our backs not to get shot by snipers or stoned by angry mobs."

"I remember this particular Saturday as if it was yesterday. The town was waking up and people begun opening their shops when suddenly three bombs exploded. Three buildings had been destroyed and innumerable casualties left behind. Then other bombs exploded in various neighborhoods destroying houses and stores, and killing numerous people. I rushed with my team to aid the injured and the wounded when the voice from our Control Room spoke through the radio receiver in my ear: "We have another one." They gave me the location of the unexploded bomb number six. My sergeant and I made our way there and forced ourselves into a bakery through the back door. I walked in first and found myself in an empty room about thirty five square feet. Before me was the counter, probably where they sold bread and pastry on any other day. I looked outside through the window at the line of houses stretching out before me. The doors of these houses opened directly onto the street and every door was ajar with a person's head peering around it and staring in my direction."

"I had a bad feeling and instantly turned to shout "Get out!" to my sergeant who was coming in behind me, but I never got to speak these words. In a flash, several bombs exploded next to me. The detonation demolished the bakery, stripped the linings off the walls, collapsed the ceiling and blasted the door and the walls. The explosion picked me up in its destructive grip and thrashed me out through the windows some twenty five feet into the street. I ended up face down on the road covered with bricks, smashed wooden beams, shattered glass and a pile of rubble."

"Some of the people who were looking from behind their open doors started walking towards me. I couldn't move my body and I knew one of two things was about to happen. If these people were IRA members they would finish the work the bomb had started. If not, they would come and help me. Two men picked me up and draped me over their shoulders to one of the military patrols down the street. My mates then called an ambulance and rushed me and my sergeant to the hospital."

"On that morning I was wearing a jacket made up of laminated layers of fiberglass, its role being to protect my vital organs from flak in case of an explosion. It was exactly what it did. The detonation vaporized the outer covering of the jacket, while its back and sides were impregnated with pieces of steel, wood and fragments of glass and concrete. It literally saved my life."

"When I arrived at the hospital I realized everything had changed in my life. My hearing was gone. I requested hearing aids, but the doctors wrote me a note saying, "Sorry fella, you don't have enough hearing to amplify and hearing aids will do you no good. Get used to being profoundly deaf. It's how you're going to spend the rest of your life." I couldn't walk anymore, but I refused the wheelchair. My legs were full of shrapnel and hundreds of debris fragments pierced my muscles, knees and joints. Every step I tried to take with the crutches triggered excruciating pain. The Royal Air Force discharged me for invalidity and I relocated to New Zealand into a farm house somewhere the country."

"Some three years later, I was in the local market one day and bumped into a group of people who, upon discovering I was deaf, signaled if they could pray for my hearing to be restored. I wrote down on a napkin, "I have no eardrums," but figured they couldn't harm me by trying. "Give it a go," I signaled. They took me to a nearby house and we sat in the lounge. The laid hands on my ears and I could see their lips moving although I couldn't hear anything of what they were saying. Nothing happened. I thanked them with my hands and went to bed that night as deaf as I had been for the past three years. In the early hours of the morning, however, I was awakened by the ticking of a clock on my bedside table. *What is that?* I wondered and leapt out of bed realizing I could hear again."

"Is this a true story?" I asked Brian.

"I went to the military hospital for a checkup," he continued, "and the doctors who treated me thought I was a fraud because the Brian they'd seen some years ago had no eardrums, but mine had been completely regenerated. From being trapped in depression and loneliness, being unemployable and useless, I had a life again. That is except for the terrible pain in my legs."

"About a week later, I bumped again into the same group of people in the local market and thanked them wholeheartedly for their prayers. They jumped around shouting "Praise the Lord!" when I told them I could hear again. We chatted and rejoiced for a few minutes, but then I had an idea. If they prayed for my hearing and it was restored, could they pray for my legs to be healed? They took me to the same house and sat me in an armchair. This time I could hear their prayers. They placed their hands on my legs and asked the Lord Jesus Christ to remove the aching from my body. I didn't know what to expect but immediately I felt the pain draining down my legs and out through my feet. This was some forty years ago. I had no pain in my legs ever since."

"Did you believe in God when all of this happened?" I asked.

"My entire life I wanted nothing to do with God. My parents were not Christians and I grew up being taught that seeing is believing. Anything related to God was not part of my world view. Regardless of my ignorance, Jesus had mercy on me. He healed me and made me live again."

2.

I looked around the living room at the black and white photographs hanging on the walls, with this Royal Air Force officer once flying jet fighters and now sipping from a cup of English tea and sharing the story of how God had miraculously healed him.

"I spent the following years studying to become a minister and a servant of the Jesus Christ" he said, "and the rest is history. My ministry is focused on deliverance from demons and healing."

"Demons? This sounds like something from medieval times," I said. "Isn't it a bit too much?"

"Most people misunderstand demonic oppression with possession" he said. "Possession, which is an extremely rare phenomenon, is when a person has lost complete control over himself and demons took over his personality. Oppression or influence, however, is more common than most people believe. Oppression is when people are bounded or distressed in certain areas of their lives. Uncontrollable fears, anxiety for no reason, voices in their head, suicidal thoughts you cannot get rid of are just a few examples of oppression. The modern man does not believe evil spirits exist and some even regard my work as absolute nonsense, but I've been doing this for thirty years and I can tell you three things with absolute certainty. (1) Demons are real, (2) They don't care whether the modern man believes in them or not, (3) The modern person can have demonic influences in their life whether they call it demonic or not. The mental and behavioral patterns of many cases of demonic oppression occur widely even in the communities that do not regard them as such. Many people experience demonic oppression even while their perception, prior beliefs and interpretation of what is actually happening varies across cultural contexts."

"What do you mean by influence?" I asked. "I've heard of demons only in stories and folklore."

"Let me ask you something first" said Brian. "What is the definition of a slave?"

I searched my mind for a few seconds. "Somebody who has a master ruling over him, I guess. Who works to exhaustion, gets nothing in return and does only what his master tells him to do?"

"Let's see what the official book says," said Brian and opened The Oxford Dictionary.

"There are two definitions" he continued,

"slave [noun] = a person who is the legal property of another and is forced to obey them; or a person who is controlled by something… Similar to what you've just said."

"Jesus Christ taught people to be careful not to sin because whoever sins becomes a slave of sin. The modern man believes sin was invented by the medieval church to manipulate the masses into good behavior, but nobody asks the question, why would the church care about what you do with your life? The reality is you can do anything you want, but beware that your actions have consequences. The church teaches about sin only to prevent you and protect you from slipping into a darkness of which you know nothing about, but nobody forbids you from going there. Sin is not the invention of the church, but is ingrained into the very fabric of the universe. Repeated sin is the doorway for demons to enter into your soul and enslave you, regardless if you believe in them or not."

"I am not sure I understand," I said.

"The test of your freedom is not in doing what you want to do, but in controlling yourself from doing what you don't truly want to do. If you are not strong enough to get rid of something that you do not want in your life, it means that something stronger than you keeps you under its power. Depressed people are the slaves of depression because they cannot control it. Depression controls them and they live their life according to its moods. Addicted people lost control over their will. They do what they don't want to do because something greater than them controls their decisions and behaviors. People who live in irrational fear are controlled by it, and they are compelled to rearrange their entire life around the dictates of their master."

"It's beginning to make sense," I said.

"Come into my office," he said. "There's something I want to show you."

Brain put his worn-out Bible on the table and I sat down at his desk. He opened a drawer and pulled out a pile of pages titled "occult diagnosis."

The list spread over several pages and included among hundreds of others, practices as acupuncture, affirmations, Buddhism, chakras, crystals, hallucinogenic drugs, Eastern philosophies, enlightenment, freemasonry, horoscopes, hypnosis, meditation, mindfulness, new age, numerology, reiki, Science of Mind, shamanism, witchcraft, yoga.

"Spiritual traditions have their roots in the ancient worship of demons," said Brain and put before me another document. "Of course, practitioners call them 'deities,' but they are nothing more than demons. Not because I say so. Their very teachings proclaim the worship of multiple spirits and local gods, which obviously are the not the one God, the Creator of the universe. Also, you can know the tree by its fruit and anyone can see the effects these teachings produce in people's lives. This is what those who study and practice the occult - 'spiritual traditions' as some call them, end up with. These pages are the results of forty years of international research."

"The conclusions of the study," I read from the document, "include depression, suicidal thoughts, fear and anxiety, resistance and disgust towards the Bible, blasphemous thoughts against God and Jesus Christ, bipolar disorders, melancholic states, inability to make decisions, sense of loss of freedom, voices in your head you cannot get rid of, irritability and rage, increased sexuality."

"But these therapies and spiritual practices promote wellbeing," I said. "How come…?"

Brian sat on the couch and looked me straight in the eye.

"Imagine I handed you a paper bag of seeds on which it is written 'corn'" he continued. "If you plant them in the ground, what will these seeds produce?"

"Corn," I said.

"No," he said. "The seeds will produce exactly what the seeds intrinsically are. It doesn't matter what is written on the bag. If I give you wheat seeds in a paper bag on which it is written "corn," you will always reap wheat and never corn. Seeds do not produce according to what is written on the bag they come from, but according to what the seeds intrinsically are. The substance - the reality of the seed, is what you will reap in the end."

"You tricked me," I said.

"Words are seeds. When words are planted into your heart, they produce according their kind. On the surface, all spiritual traditions seem universally acceptable and morally right. They speak of love and light, compassion and understanding. But just like seeds in the ground, these spiritual teachings produce in people not what is written on the package, but what they are intrinsically."

"In 1975, Seraphim Rose observed that "the new spiritual man of today can browse and find any religious idea or practice that strikes his fancy, from Western to Eastern, from Sufism to satanism. The more data he stores in his head, however, the more vague his worldview becomes." His mind "is becoming more amorphous and hazy all the time." Forty years later, research shows that 33 percent of Americans regard themselves as spiritual, but not religious. They don't identify with an organized religion, but they are creating their own spirituality. The spiritual seekers pick fragments from Buddhist teachings, practices from Hinduism, take only what benefits them from the Bible but scrap the inconvenient parts, they travel to sacred places to discover themselves, meditate in ashrams, attend ceremonies in the jungles of Peru or in the pyramids of Egypt, all of this with the goal of expanding their awareness, tapping into their divine self and awakening to the universal consciousness. These are the promises of today's spirituality, but its seeds produce according to their kind and not according to the label."

"What do you mean?" I asked.

"In 2013, professor Michael King from the University College London published the results of an extensive psychological study that measured the correlation between spiritual or religions beliefs and mental health and wellbeing. Researchers inquired 7,400 people about their religious beliefs, emotional states, mental heath problems and history of drug use and addiction. The study revealed that, regardless of physical health, age, sex, ethnicity or social support, people who are "spiritual but not religious" are 50 percent more likely to have generalized anxiety disorders and

72 percent more prone to struggle with phobias. Spiritual people are 37 percent more likely to suffer from neurotic disorders, which means they have an increased tendency towards anxiety, depression, self-doubt, shyness and other negative feelings about themselves. Spiritual seekers and practitioners are 77 percent more likely to be addicted to drugs and 40 percent more likely to take psychotropic medication, the study revealed. "There is increasing evidence that people who profess spiritual beliefs in the absence of a religious framework are more vulnerable to mental disorder," Dr. King wrote in the prestigious British Journal of Psychiatry. Another scientific study performed at the University of Oxford showed that adherents of spiritual practices are high in schizotypy. By definition, schizotypy is a set of mental, emotional and behavioral effects similar to but milder than those exhibited in schizophrenia. They are associated with high levels of anxiety and depression. Dr. Rosemary Aird from the University of Queensland in Australia surveyed more than 3,700 people and discovered that modern spiritual practices wreak havoc on the mental health of the practitioners. Her research revealed that self-focused spiritual practices - the "look within" type - are correlated with higher rates of anxiety, depression, disturbed thinking patters and anti-social behaviors. Dr. Aird's findings show that people with spiritual beliefs are twice as likely to be anxious and depressed than those with traditional religious beliefs. Spiritual practices, regardless of what the authors, teachers and gurus proclaim, produce in you according to their intrinsic reality, not according to what they promise on the package."

"Spiritual cultures and traditions date back to ancient history," continued Brian, "and modern spiritual teachers did not invent anything new. They only created an amalgam of concepts and practices gathered per their convenience from spiritual practices and the religions of the world, and stirred them into the melting-pot commonly referred to as the new age. New age is a global market of pseudoscience, spirituality, religions and opinions that promise to solve our problems by bringing us into an era of personal enlightenment, spiritual awakening and mutual acceptance. New age follows what Joseph Campbell once named 'the new planetary mythology,' a belief that man is not fallen, but that he can become perfect through the process of 'spiritual growth.' The new age believes that all spiritual and religious paths lead to the same ultimate reality, which is the divine within. There is no right or wrong, no sin nor judgement, but only people free to follow their own path to reach enlightenment by aligning with 'the universal consciousness.' On a personal level, new age believers seek to 'raise their consciousness' and to 'expand their awareness' in order to understand ever increasing levels of truth. On the community level, their goal is to create world peace by merging the religions of the world under an impersonal god in a universal spirituality that doesn't offend people of any culture, tradition, creed or belief. This spirituality of the future is developed around a set of principles rather than a figure, and places man at the center in search of his own divinity. On the surface, the promise of peace and unity is commendable and the personal benefits are desirable: wellness for the body, mind and soul. In reality, however, the new age is driven by demons with the goal of turning people away from the living God."

"There are many people out there who will get offended by these words," I said.

"My words shouldn't anger anyone" replied Brian, "because it is neither me nor the Christians who say these words, but it is the very founder of the new age movement."

"How can this be?"

"The ideology of the new age movement was initially written by occultist Helen Blavatsky who founded the Theosophical Society in 1875, and later by Alice Bailey in the early 1900s. Their public goal was to create 'a universal religion of truth,' but in secret they did nothing but choose to side with evil in the most ancient of battles. Helen Blavatsky, the founder of theosophy, which is the very root of the modern new age movement, confessed to be a worshipper of Satan."

Brian searched for a piece of paper on his desk and read it to me. "In 1888, Blavatsky wrote in her book *The Secret Doctrine*: "That which the clergy of every dogmatic religion - preeminently Christian - points out as Satan, the enemy of God, is in reality the highest divine spirit. Thus, it is but natural to view Satan, the serpent of Genesis, as the real creator and benefactor, the father of spiritual mankind."

Why get offended with Christianity when we say the new age is demonic when the very founder of the new age movement wrote down in her own words that the root of her teaching is Satan?

Why would people get angry with Christians for plainly telling them what their founder has hid from them? Can you see now why new age believers accept anything and everything, *except* Jesus Christ as their Lord and Savior? Do you understand now why new agers welcome every teaching and mystical book - The Bhagavad Gita, Tao Te Ching, The Tibetan Book of the Dead, the Vedas, Sutras and all other, *except* the Bible? According to Blavatsky, the purpose of the Theosophical Society is to "oppose the materialism of science and every form of dogmatic theology, especially the Christian, which the chiefs of the society regard as particularly pernicious."

"Christianity is particularly dangerous for them," I commented.

"Isn't this interesting?" Brian continued. "The great majority of modern new age seekers believe Satan is not real, but the very founder of the new age philosophy praises Satan in her books - the same Satan that spiritual people dismiss as a manipulation of the church. How is it that new age believers accept and embrace every spiritual and religious tradition except the Bible and yet the founder of the new age movement worships the Satan described in the very Bible in which they declare they do not believe because it is corrupted? Do you begin to see the deception behind the new age? If there weren't any Jesus Christ or Christianity, the new age would still be founded on the source of all evil."

"Meanwhile, people who struggle to find healing and some sense of peace in their life buy in a pretty package the seed of the oldest deception in the world - worshipping demons. If the very founder of the movement that promises freedom, enlightenment and unity is a self-proclaimed devil worshipper, what else is left to think about? Libraries upon libraries of spiritual books flow from one source, Satan, the devil of the Bible. If the seed is evil, is it a mystery that its fruits are evil too? Seeds always produce according to their intrinsic reality."

"People spend millions of dollars each year on spiritual books," I noted. "They're everywhere."

"Nobody would pay for and practice something that promises mental problems, guarantees depression, comes with emotional torment, leads to broken marriages and even suicide. Spiritual practices have been wrapped up in packages that promise life, but hold only death inside. Satan is the father of all lies and in him there is no truth. Therefore, why is it surprising that the label promises freedom and wellbeing, but its harvest is only bondage and affliction?"

"The apostle Peter wrote about these modern teachers in the Bible saying "they promise them freedom, while they themselves are slaves of depravity." When you get entangled in the new age, it is very difficult to be set free, and more and more people are seeing these effects in their lives."

"In the early 1970s, the new age philosophy was only for the initiated few, but these ideas and practices have infused more and more into all spheres of human activity, leading into darkness millions of people who, in all sincerity, are only looking for a better life and do not know what is behind these principles. It is not being evil that injures you, but ignorance and lack of wisdom. These days, the new age principles have become a leaven hid in every area of our lives - psychology, sociology, healthcare, education, business and government. Mental hospitals have instituted new age programs that include Eastern meditations, spiritual psychology and others of the like. People all over the world practice yoga and have adopted Ayurvedic medicine as ways to promote wholeness and wellbeing. Yoga has grown out a need for health, but the seed of what they are doing, whether they know it or not, is the ritualistic worship of Hindu deities. You cannot separate the practice from the underlying philosophy. Organizations are investing millions of dollars in new age programs for employees - hypnosis, guided meditations, positive thinking, psychic healing, mind control. Some public schools have introduced meditation as means of 'inner healing' for children. This wave of spiritual deception is so subtle that even churches and synagogues have adopted meditation practices and mindfulness techniques. Behind the new age, however, is nothing but the seed of demons bearing fruit not in "light and compassion" according to their promise, but in confusion, mental problems and emotional hurt according to their intrinsic reality. Satan is the god of this world, therefore do not be surprised to discover that the new age teachings are completely opposite to what Jesus Christ taught."

what the world teaches	what Jesus teaches
Believe in yourself.	Believe in God, believe in Me.
Look within.	Look unto Jesus Christ.
Trust yourself.	Trust God.
You can do anything.	Without Me you can do nothing.
There is no sin.	Sin leads to death.
Love yourself.	Love God. Love one another.
Religions are different paths leading to God.	Nobody comes to the Father but through Me.
Nurture your inner child.	Grow up, mature yourself in Christ.
The Universe provides.	"Even to your old age and gray hairs I am He, I am He who will sustain you. I have made you and I will carry you; I will sustain you."
You are free to call God anything you want: Source, universe, infinite energy, divine light.	Jesus is the name to which everything in the universe will bow. There is no other name given to mankind by which we are saved.

"Since the first century AD, the apostles of Jesus Christ have warned us about the days ahead and wrote "the Spirit [of God] expressly says that in latter times some will depart from the faith, giving heed to deceiving spirits and doctrines of demons." Demons are not creatures with tails and pitchforks, but spiritual entities with a mind, emotions and will of their own, who oppress people with the sole purpose of destroying the humanity who God so dearly loves.

3.

On May 6, 1953, police officers picked up from the streets of Manila, seventeen-year-old Clarita Villanueva and put her in Bilibid prison for vagrancy. Clarita's parents had died when she was only a child and she had come to Manila, the capital city of the Philippines, to earn a living as a maid. Four days after she was arrested, Clarita, an otherwise soft spoken and polite girl, begun screaming in terror in her cell before the eyes of the inmates and prison officers. She claimed that she had been attacked and bitten by two demons, and showed officers the fresh bites on her arms. The officer on duty informed his superiors and the case became public.

In the following days, Clarita was bitten several times on her right knee, arms, shoulders and neck. Medical doctors, experts and psychiatrists examined Clarita, but could not agree on the cause of the phenomenon. A medical staff member of the Manila Police Department diagnosed the girl as plainly insane and claimed that she had probably bit herself during epileptic seizures. The army psychiatrist of the Armed Forces of the Philippines Medical Center put forth the view that Clarita was suffering from "hysterical fugue." Another medical authority dismissed the case as mere malnutrition. The doctors were skeptical and believed the girl was biting herself.

"Clarita talked and answered questions weakly before a crowd of observers," wrote the local newspaper *The Daily Mirror* on May 12. But then "suddenly, her facial expressions would change to anguish and horror," and she would scream as if attacked by an invisible enemy. *The Manila Chronicle* reported on May 13 that "at least twenty-five competent persons, including Manila's Chief of Police Colonel Cesar Lucero, [declare] that it is a very realistic example of a horrified woman being bitten to insanity by 'invisible persons.' She displayed several bite marks all over her body inflicted by nobody as far as the twenty-five witnesses could see. All witnesses agree that she was never able to bite herself." Nobody can bite their own neck.

Dr. Mariano B. Lara, Head of the Department of Pathology and Legal Medicine at the Manila Central University and professor of Legal Medicine at University of Santo Tomas was the Chief Medical Examiner in charge of Clarita's case. In 38 years of medical practice, Dr. Lara performed more than 8,000 autopsies and had never accepted anything on the lines of a spiritual reality. Clarita's case however, changed his philosophy of life.

"My first notice of Clarita Villanueva, Bilibid prison cell inmate," writes Dr. Lara in the official case report, "was on May 11, [1953]. Upon arriving at my office at the city morgue, I was met by Dr. Abelardo Lucero, [who] reported that he had seen human teeth-like impressions on both arms of the girl, but believed that these impressions were likely the effects of her own biting. I paid no special attention to this report, considering it of little or no consequence. My years of training as a doctor are only scientific [and] I find it difficult, nearly impossible to accept anything of a supernatural character." Dr. Lucero recommended Clarita to be hospitalized in the National Psychopathic Hospital and Dr. Lara signed the regular form diagnosing the girl as epileptic predisposed to depressive attacks. Clarita, however, remained in jail.

On May 13, Dr. Lara continues, "I returned to my office" where thirty medical interns who were finishing their doctorate degrees under his supervision at the University of Santo Tomas had "already gathered for their class." At Dr. Lara's request, Clarita was brought by ambulance to his office. When the girl arrived, "she was unconscious and was carried into my observation room seated in a chair. She was placed in front of the class of interns and myself. Clarita's body was soft and entirely insensitive to all stimuli. Her arms lifted by me would fall without resistance. Pointed needles and pens touching her skin gave no response throughout her body surface. After several minutes in this condition, Clarita began to come out of this state of insensibility and trance." Alfonso Aquino, a morgue technician, took the girl from the chair and placed her on a bed when suddenly she screamed and told Aquino: "[The bite] is under your hand." Aquino removed his hand and in Clarita's hand, under his palm "were teeth marks that were still moist with saliva and sinking into the skin," testified Dr. David Cabreira who was present in the room at the time. "When I removed Alfonso's hand from Clarita's," continues Lara, "I saw with my unbelieving eyes the clear marks of human-like teeth from both the upper and lower jaws. It was a little moist in the bitten area. I could not understand nor explain how they were produced as her hand had all the time been held away from the reach of her mouth, and that the place where the bite-impressions occurred, on the dorsal on the left hand, was the very place held by my assistant Alfonso. I knew she could not bite herself nor could Alfonso, who does not possess a single tooth, having recently had them extracted by a dentist. I am also sure that I did not bite the girl causing the impressions to appear on her hand! Clarita kept on screaming for about fifteen minutes and she turned bluish in the face and legs as if being choked." Reddish bite marks appeared on her neck and "after about twenty minutes of the attack, accompanied by stiffness and screaming, her body became soft and in a trance-like condition." One university professor, one medical doctor and a team of thirty doctoral students witnessed this event and could not find "any possible explanation insofar as my human experience in medical training is concerned," Dr. Lara concluded.

The national media aimed to expose Clarita's case as a fraud. Reporters from the Philippines Free Press, the oldest English language periodical in the country, visited Bilibid prison some days later escorted by Dr. Abelardo Lucero of the Manila Police Medico-Legal Department. "Just as we were mounting the steps of the concrete building," reporters wrote, "we were startled by blood-curling screams from within. In the cell we found Clarita seated on a wooden bed with tears still flowing down her cheeks. A civilian, [whom we later learned was American Christian evangelist Dr. Lester Sumrall] was kneeling on the cement floor before the girl. He was holding both of Clarita's hands by the writs and praying." Reporters noted that Dr. Lara was standing on one side, wiping tears away from his own eyes. Behind him was prison officer captain Antonio Ganibi, who stood there speechless and Dr. Dominga Reyes, professor of psychology and philosophy at a local university. Dr. Lara took Clarita's left arm and trembled as he pointed another fresh bite on it. News reporters drew closer and looked at the bite. "The sight sent a cold shiver down our spine" they testified. "It did not, in any way, resemble a human bite. It was too large for human teeth and the bite was completely round, as if made by molars only."

The voice coming out Clarita's mouth cursed Lester Sumrall who continued to pray, cursed God and the blood of Jesus Christ. She cursed in English, although Clarita couldn't speak English. "Clarita," Dr. Sumrall said as he pulled a chair in front of her and took her by the hand, "I have come to deliver you from the power of these devils in the name of Jesus Christ, the Son of God." Suddenly, Clarita went into a fit of rage. "No! No!" she screamed, "they will kill me!" Her body became rigid and she became unconscious. Sumrall took her head with both hands and shouted "Come out of her you evil and wicked spirit of hell! Come out of her in Jesus' name!" Instantly, she regained consciousness and began to rage again. She cursed God, cursed Jesus Christ and the Holy Spirit in the foulest language. Hours later, "with tears flowing down her cheeks, she begged me to leave her alone and showed me terrible marks on her arms and neck where she had been bitten in that moment. I was shocked," recalls Sumrall. "Some of the small blood vessels underneath the skin were broken."

The following day Sumrall returned to continue his prayers of deliverance and requested every person present to kneel. "I warned them not to mock or laugh," he remembers, "for when the devils come out of Clarita they would surely attack another victim. Doctors, newspapermen, police officers and [university] professors humbly knelt as I prayed." However, in the next cell, there was a woman prisoner jesting about the event, and when Clarita was delivered, she was bitten and immediately fell unconscious. Her story came out in the newspapers in the same day.

Sumrall commanded the demons to come out of Clarita in the name of Jesus Christ and after some time, "I felt the release that they had departed," he recalls. "Clarita relaxed." The demonized expression departed from her eyes and she smiled. "I looked around and saw newspapermen had been weeping. There were tears in the eyes of doctors, otherwise hard-boiled jailers were weeping." Clarita was set free.

She became normal, was released from prison, and moved to a small town away from the public attention. Her story is documented in Dr. Lester Sumrall's book *Bitten by Devils*.

4.

"Brian, you're a former Royal Air Force officer" I said. "What does your skeptical brain say about all this?"

"If you don't believe my words," he said, "believe the science. Some of the most distinguished scientists and mental health researchers are beginning to discover the reality of demons. Dr. Richard Gallagher is a professor of psychiatry at the New York Medical College, faculty at Columbia University and an award winning, board-certified psychiatrist in New York. He was educated in psychiatry at Yale University, trained in psychoanalysis at Columbia University and has treated more than 25,000 patients in his counseling career spanning over several decades. He encountered several cases in his practice that he could only explain as demonic. "If you are knowledgeable about this field [of demonic oppression]," writes Gallagher, "you have to come to the conclusion that the most likely explanation is that *evil spirits are a scientific fact.*"

Dr. William P. Wilson, professor emeritus of psychiatry at Duke University Medical Center, a prestigious institution by any standards in the scientific world, regards many of the mental problems attributed to demons as purely psychological, but he also concluded there are rare yet very real cases of demonic possession. He gives an example he encountered of a woman whose parents practiced the occult. She "would be violently thrown to the floor, whereupon two male voices" would speak through her in another language. Dr. Wilson commanded the spirits to leave her in the name of Jesus Christ, and she immediately regained normal behavior and remained healthy thereafter. "There is little belief in a supernatural kingdom of evil," Wilson wrote in a peer-reviewed scientific journal. "Satan's chief weapon is to convince the world that he does not exist. Science has believed him. The result is that mental health workers are unable to recognize or treat demon possession when it occurs. To recognize demon possession a person must possess the ability to discern the spirits and have diagnostic criteria that allow positive diagnosis."

In 1983, world-renowned Harvard-educated psychiatrist M. Scott Peck shocked the psychiatric community by describing his participation in two exorcisms. Peck wrote that the two persons "were gravely ill from a psychiatric standpoint before their exorcisms" but "after the exorcisms the mental state of these patients was dramatically improved." Following additional psychotherapy, the voices in their heads died out and both patients made a full recovery. Similar to other respected professionals, Peck dismissed most supposed demonic oppressions as nothing but psychological problems, but also acknowledged he encountered cases that could only be explained as demonic. He became so convinced of this reality that he risked his entire professional career and recommended the need for exorcisms despite the scorn he received from the medical community. Peck declared that there is enough empirical evidence already available today "to make demonology a respectable field of research and study."

Father Vince Lampert, a pastor and exorcist from the United States, also acknowledges that "true cases of demonic possession are extremely rare." The Church, however, does have a protocol to determine if someone is mentally ill, but if doctors can't find evidence that the person has a medical condition, then he looks for signs of the demonic.

"We should use the word possession only when it fits - for the rare Charles Mansons of the world," wrote Dr. Francis MacNutt in 1995. MacNutt summarizes what happens when an oppressing spirit or spirits are being delivered from a victim in three categories: "bodily contortions, changes in the voice, and changes in facial expression." Spirit victims sometimes exhibit supernatural strength. They "may arch their spines backward, while still others roll on the ground." Furthermore, "the tone of the person's voice changes. A woman may start speaking in a husky voice like a man, or a mild-mannered person may begin speaking in a snide, insulting tone of voice." Often the voice uses the plural *we* and on rare occasions speaks in a foreign language. "Perhaps the most common external indication of demonization" continues MacNutt, "comes when the person's facial expression changes. It is as if you are not longer looking at the same person you started speaking to. The old saying, "the eyes are the windows of the soul" becomes especially meaningful. It is as if the evil spirit is peering out at you. The eyes become filled with hate, mockery, pride, or whatever the nature of that particular spirit is."

David Van Gelder Ph.D., while noting that most claims of demonic possession are false, he also presented in a professional journal a real case he encountered in his practice. When a sixteen-year-old boy involved with the occult started "snarling like an animal," his father, a physician himself, considered that the boy was demon-possessed and requested a team of pastors and mental health professionals to help. A minister asked the boy to repeat "Jesus Christ, Son of God," but before the young man could finish saying these words, his visage and his voice altered. "You fools," came out through his mouth, "he can't say that." Several of those present were professionals. This case is similar to an account from the time of Jesus documented in *The*

Gospel of Mark. "Suddenly, a man in the synagogue who was possessed by an evil spirit cried out, "Why are you interfering with us, Jesus of Nazareth? Have you come to destroy us? I know who you are—the Holy One of God!" But Jesus reprimanded him. "Be quiet! Come out of the man," he ordered. At that, the evil spirit screamed, threw the man into a convulsion, and then came out of him. Amazement gripped the audience, and they began to discuss what had happened."

Another psychiatrist, Grant Mullen, M.D., was shocked to hear an unfamiliar voice coming from a patient, insisting "Let her alone, she's ours!" Mullen reported that something supernatural seemed to be happening for which most mental health professionals are not trained. He succeeded in expelling the spirits by invoking the name of Jesus Christ.

"It is impossible to avoid arriving at the surprising conclusion that evil spirits are real and that they sometimes obsess and possess the living. For if they were not real, why would an exorcism work?" writes Dr. Stafford Betty in an academic journal. "Is it not reasonable to conclude that exorcism works so dramatically, completely and permanently in cases where conventional psychiatry fails because the exorcist has correctly diagnosed the ailment and the psychiatrist has not?" Dr. Ralph Alllison, a psychotherapist specialized in multiple personality disorder writes, "Despite all my efforts," in some cases "I was unable to find a more plausible explanation for [the] existence of [a personality] than the spirit theory. Francis MacNutt recalls, "I once prayed for a young woman who had been confined in a mental hospital for twelve years, suffering from schizophrenia. After two hours of prayer for healing and deliverance, the glazed look in her eyes left and she was able to converse in a normal way. Several weeks later the doctors recognized a dramatic change in her behavior and released her from the hospital." Dr. Scott Peck recommended that exorcism is the only effective cure in certain situations. "Difficult and dangerous though they were, the exorcisms I witnessed were successful," he writes. "I have every reason to believe that had they not had their exorcisms, they would each be dead by now."

More and more highly respected and reputable mental health professionals are opening up to the reality of the demonic, although not many are open to talking about it. Dr. Jeffrey Lieberman,

Director of the New York State Psychiatric Institute arrived at a similar conclusion. He recalled a case he had experienced which left him "completely freaked out." This was basically a battle between the doctors and "whatever it was that afflicted the individual." Asked whether he ruled out demonic possession, Dr Lieberman replied: "No. There was no way I could explain what happened." Dr. Lewis-Fernández, president-elect of the World Association of Cultural Psychiatry is working to include the diagnosis of "possession" in the Diagnostic and Statistical Manual of Mental Disorders (DSM). The DSM is the cornerstone of modern psychiatric practice and the handbook relied upon by medical clinicians, researchers and the international legal system. Dr. Mark J. Albanese of the Cambridge Health Alliance is a psychiatrist who studied medicine at Cornell University and has been practicing psychiatry for decades. In a letter for the New Oxford Review, he wrote: "There's a certain openness to experiences that are happening that are beyond what we can explain by MRI scans, neurobiology or even psychological theories. Possession is very rare. Much more common is subtle satanic influence."

Psychiatrist Walter C. Johnson acknowledges that most emotional problems are illnesses, but he had also seen in his practice a few clear cases of demonic possession. All these patients have been involved with the occult. Another psychiatrist observed about 280 cases that required deliverance from demons, especially resulting from dabbling in occult practices such as Ouija boards, horoscopes and witchcraft. "The most common cause [for demonic oppression]," Dr. Gallagher concluded, "is someone has turned to evil or the occult." For the skeptics who wonder how a scientifically trained medical doctor can believe "such outdated and scientific nonsense," Gallagher gives a simple answer. "I honestly weigh the evidence." You can refute something only if you have knowledge in the field, but if you don't have any knowledge, how can you deny what you know nothing about? "The thing about skeptics is - the extreme skeptics - they've never seen a case," says Gallagher. "Contrary to what secular opinion asserts, an objective medical view can confidently conclude that assaults by the devil, like genuine miracles, are rare but quite *real scientific facts*, verifiable to all who are not afraid to confront the truth."

5.

"What can be more dangerous than for somebody to knock at the door of your house as an innocent lamb when your teenage girl is alone by herself and walk inside as a ravaging wolf?" Brian continued. "Yet this is what's been happening beginning with year 2000 since witchcraft practices have dramatically increased among the youth. Disguised in innocent fairytales and fantasy, mainstream movies and books lure young people into occult rituals, black magic and real figures from the history of witchcraft. Witchcraft is spreading more and more among the youth as teens are tempted with how powerful they can become through occult knowledge and practices. Witchcraft has actually become the top interest among teenage girls in the Western world."

"In 2001, the Pagan Federation of England recorded a rising number of queries from young people. "We have a huge surge of calls, mostly from young girls," declared their media officer and attributed the youth's growing interest in sorcery to mainstream novels and films that make witchcraft seem cool and attractive. In a study across thousands of students in schools across the U.K., researchers found that 54 percent of teens are "interested" in the occult and 26 percent are "very interested." Trinity College and Pew Research Center ran several studies in the United States and discovered that the number of Wicca practitioners grew from an estimated 8,000 people in 1990, to 340,000 in 2008, to almost 1.5 million in 2014. Wicca is a popular form of witchcraft introduced to the general public in 1900s by Gerald Gardner who was initiated into a coven of witches and worshipped "the horned god." There's a lot of smoke and mirrors about modern witchcraft practices, but if you pierce through the veil with a critical eye, you will always find behind them the oldest enemy of humanity - Satan of the Bible. Of course, most dismiss witchcraft as merely the fantasy of an imaginary world, but bear in mind that people suffer not because they are evil, but because they lack knowledge. Jesus told people, "My words are full of Spirit and life." He came to sow the seed of God into our hearts. Then, what else but death can Satan's words be full of? The Bible tells us that "the very essence of God's words is truth." Therefore, what else but lies is the essence of the words of demons? It doesn't matter if people regard witchcraft as mere stories for teenagers to tickle their fancy, because once they are planted in your heart, whether you know what you are planting or not, the seeds always produce according to their intrinsic reality."

Brian pulled out a large file from his desk drawer filled with newspapers clippings.

"Judge for yourself," he said and passed me the documents. I started reading:

The New York Times, April 22, 2016: "U.S. suicide rate surges to a 30-year high."

Chicago Tribune, April 22, 2016: "U.S. suicide rate surges to three decade high."

CBS News, November 21, 2017: "What's behind the rise in youth suicides?"

The Wall Street Journal, May 15, 2018: "Youth suicidal behavior is on the rise, especially among girls."

Time, May 16, 2018: "More kids are attempting and thinking about suicide."

Centers for Disease Control and Prevention, June 7, 2018: "Suicide rates rising across the U.S."

USA Today, March 19, 2019: "Teen suicide is soaring."

"The U.S. Government recently alarmed people that suicide rates had jumped by 30 percent between 2000 and 2016. This rise is especially dramatic among young girls between 10 and 14 years old."

Business Insider, June 14, 2018: "The U.S. suicide rate has tripled for young girls since 2000."

"The suicide rate among teenage girls in 2018 was nearly three times higher than in year 2000. While the overall number of suicides has dropped between 2010 and 2017, during the same period the number of teenage suicides has increased by 67 percent. A study published in the prestigious *Journal of the American Medical Association* in 2018 showed that self-inflicted injury rates for teenage girls 10 to 14 years old increased by almost 20 percent every year between 2009 and 2015. Scientists believe these numbers are underestimated because many of the cases remain unreported. "These findings are consistent with previously documented upward trends in youth suicide rates between 1999 and 2014, and coincide with increased reports of depression among the youth, especially young girls," the study revealed. If you plot the data about the increase of witchcraft and the data on self-inflicted harm and suicide among the youth, they rise along each other. Repeated coincidence in science is called correlation or causation."

Dr. Kurt Koch, a German theologian who traveled to more than one hundred countries and lectured on every continent on Earth, discovered that "more than 60 percent of mental disorders are caused by practicing and being involved in the occult." Dr. James Cloud, licensed mental health practitioner and archbishop in the Advent Catholic Church warns that the modern society, with its interest in drugs, ouija boards, new age, witchcraft and the occult is fueling the need to perform more deliverances from demons. He adds that as "years go by, the cases are getting darker" and keep rising in number. In the United States, according to theologian Malachi Martin, there was a "750 percent increase in the number of exorcisms performed between the early 1960s and the mid 1970s." In England, Dom Robert Petitpierre, editor of the Anglican "Exeter Report" on exorcism found that "incidents of demonic interference have become virtually an explosion since 1960." But in spite of the increase in mental and emotional problems, self-inflicted harm and suicide rates, "the vast majority [of people still] think that spirits - at least the kind that oppress or possess us are not real," notes Dr. Stafford Betty of the California State University."

"The problem is that the less people know about demons, the more control they have on our society. Satan functions in ignorance" Brian continued. "It breaks my heart to see how far people have ventured from their relationship with God. The only way to abundant life, absolute freedom and overflowing love is to have a heart-to-heart, sincere relationship with Jesus Christ. Consider this. If you have a child, do you want him to chant, rub bowls, light sticks, twist his body in strange positions or take drugs in order to talk to you, or do you want your child to come to you with an open heart, in total trust of your love for him? Don't you want him to tell you the truth no matter what is on his heart and ask for help with the confidence that you are always there for him? You don't need man-made techniques to talk to the One who made you. Talk to Jesus Christ in spirit and in truth, and he will answer you. The dead don't talk, but Jesus is alive and he answers your prayers.

I want to make something very clear so that there is no room left for misunderstandings or debate. The exclusive way for you to be in the presence of God is Jesus Christ. Until you come to him you don't know this, although in your mind you think you do. Every other way is from the evil one and leads to death. Come to Jesus because everything you need is found in him."

CHAPTER 5

To Stand Before Him

Q5 - Where is Jesus Christ today?

*"The whole of science is nothing more than
a refinement of everyday thinking" - Albert Einstein*

1.

I drove my twenty-year-old car along the Pacific coast, then veered right and climbed into the hills through orchards of avocados, kiwi fruit and citrus trees. The car fumed its way up into the mountains past mansions, wild lands and ranches. In the distance, the peaks disappeared under rainclouds rolling dark and steaming down the forest. I parked on the gravel road in front of the wooden house and danged the copper bell hanging by the door.

Mary, our host, was born in Europe, but her family had moved to America when she was only a child. Now in her early 70s, she was living with her husband on a property overlooking an exquisite flower garden and the rainforest beyond. The two of them had transformed part of their land into a botanical garden filled with flowers and fragrances from every corner of the world, while the other half remained a native forest with innumerable species of birds who found their home in the branches. The only track going through the forest led down to a bend in a river, a secret oasis cropped out from the garden of paradise where Mary was swimming every day in summer. Her pure white hair flowed down to her shoulders and she beheld me through two blue eyes infused with gentleness.

"There's something special I would like to show you tonight," she said. "See me after dinner."

When darkness fell upon the mountain and after the dog was fed and locked inside for the night, Mary got two winter jackets and a torch, and bid me to walk with her on the property. We swathed ourselves with the coats and descended on the mud pathway through the forest following the beam of light in front of us. The river was rustling in the valley below and our steps swooshed rhythms in the silence of the night. We hiked for maybe fifteen minutes, before Mary stopped and turned off the torch.

"This is the place," she whispered in my direction.

I blinked a couple of times to adjust to the absolute darkness, but then I looked down to discover what seemed a multitude of stars spreading across the ground everywhere around us. It seemed as if the galaxies had fallen from the sky and we were treading on stars beneath our feet.

"What are these…?" I whispered worried not to scare them away.

We were surrounded by millions of tiny dots of light below us and above, as if the earth had become a mirror held up to the night sky.

"They're glow worms," said Mary. "Isn't this wonderful?"

"I've never seen anything like this," I said. "It's as if all the stars had fallen in your garden."

"God had spilled a galaxy in the forest," Mary said laughing.

We stood in silence for a while.

"Do you know that just as tonight my garden is a reflection of the sky above," Mary continued, "in the same way our lives on earth are nothing but mere shadows of heaven, a dim reflection of the glorious reality waiting for us above?"

"I'm not sure I follow" I said.

"I would like to tell you a story," Mary continued and walked slowly along the path.

"Thirty years ago my husband and I took our children to explore the native forest in the mountain ranges surrounding our property. He was tramping ahead on the track with our oldest son and I followed behind with our daughter. We were laughing and singing, holding hands under the summer sun when all of a sudden a bee stung me in the back of my neck. I only had a moment to tell my girl to run and get her father before I collapsed in the dirt. I fought to keep my eyes open, but I couldn't. Everything went dark. All of a sudden I found myself traveling up through a tunnel, faster than I ever imagined possible, and moving towards a brilliant light shinning brighter than a million suns somewhere in the distance. Rays of light and living colors, voices as of angels and heavenly music swirled around me and blended with me.

"Mary!" I heard a voice calling my name from nowhere and yet from everywhere. The whole atmosphere was infused with dazzling colors as of many rainbows and exuded a fragrance of flowers I never breathed before. Surreal colors and living light weaved together with what seemed to be songs of worship and praise. Everything radiated with glory and color and life.

"Mary," called me again the voice from the light.

I had never felt such joy, serenity and peace.

"Mary," the voice spoke again. I was physically soaked in golden liquid love.

"Mary!" somebody shouted. "Mary, do you hear me? Come back!"

I opened my eyes to see a nurse slapping me inside of an ambulance.

Rage flared through my veins when I realized the medical staff had brought me back from where I was. I had no idea what I had experienced, but all I wanted was to stay in that place of glory and majesty, serenity and peace. They rushed me to the hospital and put me back on my feet in a couple of days. The experience lingered in my memory and I longed to return to that place, but time passed and I eventually resumed my daily living, writing for the local newspaper and raising our two children."

"That is for a few years until our daughter passed away. When she was only twelve, our girl died from an asthma attack in our arms, before our very eyes. Everything changed for us. If you don't have children you cannot understand what breaks inside a parent's heart when their child dies. When your husband dies, you are called a widow. When you parents die, you are called an orphan. But when you child dies, there is no word to define the sorrow. We still had her brother to raise, and this is what kept us going. But my nights were never the same. After everyone went to bed, I locked myself in the office and spent countless hours investigating everything I could about death and dying. Questions flooded my mind, such as "What happens to us when we die?" "Where is my little girl now?" "What did I experience years before when I went through the tunnel of light toward that place of glory and love? Was it just a fantasy, a hallucination of my dying brain grasping for its life, or is there another reality waiting for us in the afterlife?"

The wind through the forest and the sounds of the night stood still as Mary spoke.

"Let's go back to the house," she continued. "There is something I want to show you."

Mary turned on the lamp and sat in her wooden chair, while I sank in a couch in the corner of the room. Shelves of books covered three of the four walls of her study. When Mary spoke, in the yellow light of the lamp I noticed dust particles flying off the pile of papers, handwritten notes, newspaper clippings and pages torn from old books now carefully arranged on her desk. She put the eyeglasses on her nose, and picked a leftover pencil from a jar filled with crayons.

"Science, by definition," said Mary, "is the activity of studying the natural world through observation. Observations are the lifeblood of scientific inquiry. In matters of science, more observations lead to more accurate conclusions. If you don't have any facts or observations, or if for whatever reason you reject the facts you have, then there is no science. Linus Pauling, Nobel prize laureate once said that "facts are the air of scientists. Without them you can never fly.""

Mary crayoned a square on a piece of paper and then traced vertical and horizontal lines to divide it into many tiny squares. "A scientific investigation is similar to building a puzzle," she said. "If you have only a few pieces," and she filled a couple of squares, "it is impossible to form the complete picture. But if you have many pieces of data," and she crayoned all but a few squares on the page, "you come closer to the reality of what the picture really is. Even if some pieces are still missing, the more data you have the more you can understand about reality."

"I have been long enough on this earth to know that sometimes, if you want to discover the truth about something, is best to put aside other people's opinions and look at the data yourself. Study the facts with your own mind, create the puzzle yourself, and draw the conclusion with your own wisdom. The beginning of my research in trying to answer the questions I had about death was disappointing. I found nothing but a clash of opinions, some scientists saying near-death experiences are mere hallucinations, other experts declaring there is an afterlife. I'd been an investigative journalist my entire life, I needed the facts and the data and not other people's opinions. Therefore, I scraped everything I had heard and begun my investigation from scratch. The first question I asked was "What are the observations regarding the dying? What was the actual data saying about near-death experiences?"

"The term near-death experience (NDE) was introduced in the scientific literature in the 1970s. Near-death experiences are personal accounts associated with death or impending death, and take place during life-threatening situations. These accounts are reported by people who come close to death when many of them are surrounded by high-tech medical devices measuring everything possible about the human body. Medical technology continues to improve and doctors can resuscitate people from even further into the realms of death. From a materialistic medical point of view, near-death experiences should be impossible because they occur when people have no heartbeat and no brain activity, they are unconscious in a coma or clinically dead."

"In spite of being flatlined on the operating table or trapped in a car wreck, drowned in a river or murdered in a violent assault, in surgery under anesthesia or in cardiac arrest, thousands upon thousands of people return to report clear and lucid experiences. Research at the University of Virginia shows that near-death experiencers testify being highly aware and very much alive during their NDE. They think with greater clarity and faster than usual, and are more conscious and more alert during the NDE than they are in normal life. Some of them testify floating above their body and witnessing their surroundings before rushing through a dark tunnel towards a brilliant light. Some experience a life review with a being of light and recall important events to learn how their actions and behaviors have influenced other people. Others meet and have brief conversations with deceased family members. NDErs often recall being in a realm bubbling with life, with dazzling light and surreal colors, feeling incredible peace and belonging, perfect safety and overwhelming love. Then the moment comes when either by choice of by force they return to the body. I remember myself going through that tunnel with glorious colors blending together with a surreal music after the bee stung me, but I was brought back and didn't experience anything else. Therefore, I had to research the data."

"Near-death experiences are more common than most people imagine," Mary continued and pulled out a black book from the shelves behind her. "In the 1970s, NDE accounts were discarded as delusions produced by a dying brain, but they are now studied in mainstream science as authentic experiences. Thousands of near-death accounts have been reviewed according to scientific standards in specialized medical literature. *The Handbook of Near-Death Experiences - Thirty Years of Investigation* is a review book written by medical doctors and university professors that documents more than 600 academic articles and 3,500 cases explored in peer-reviewed scientific journals. In the United States alone, an average of 700 adults go through an NDE each day, which means about 200,000 people die and return to tell the story every year. The data is generous for research, with more than 10 million people having had an NDE since 1992. Scientists continue to accumulate evidence in support of NDEs being real journeys into the afterlife, thus demonstrating that NDEs are actually a common human experience. Scholars have worked for four decades to provide insights into the afterlife and any of the books on the topic will enlighten you on the science supporting them. My goal, however, was to answer three totally different questions."

2.

"Before he was crucified," Mary continued, "Jesus Christ told his disciples "I have come down from heaven. I came from the Father and entered the world, now I am leaving the world and going back to the Father who is in heaven." Apostle Paul also wrote that Jesus literally lives in heaven. I wanted to believe these words, but I had find out if science can verify what the Bible is saying. Is there any data?"

"Therefore, my first question was, "according to the observations, is there a heaven?" John Burke, engineer and author of the book *Imagine Heaven* has spent thirty years studying more than one thousand near-death experiences. He studied in detail NDE accounts of people from different countries and cultures, adults and children, professionals and academics, businessmen, airline pilots, neurosurgeons, men and women from all walks of life, and discovered that their experiences in the afterlife follow a similar pattern. Immediately after dying, NDErs become aware of their new spiritual body and find themselves in an environment of brilliant light and radiating love. Sometimes they encounter relatives or friends who passed on before them, and they communicate with each other in perfect understanding. Thousands of testimonies reveal that heaven is a real place, infused with life, majesty and glory. According to the data, heaven is more beautiful, more exquisite and more real than anything on earth."

"How are the testimonies of people actual data?" I said.

"Think of it this way. In 1969 three astronauts landed on the moon, a place nobody has seen before. They returned home and told the story. Of course, even with the photographs they took, we do not know for sure whether what they said was true, a mixture of truth and lies, or a complete deception. But as more people walked on the surface of the moon, their stories begun to give us a more accurate picture of reality. More pieces from a puzzle, more knowledge about the actual image. Now imagine if thousands of people every day could walk on the moon and return to tell their story. Although their testimonies would vary in details, depending on their memory, personal interests and local experience, major lies are washed out and a true image of reality emerges. By itself, a testimony cannot be called science. Today, however, we have thousands, possibly tens of thousands of near-death experiences recorded over the course of the last forty years. Their number is so overwhelming that they become data, and we can infer patterns and draw reliable conclusions," said Mary.

"My second question was, "according to the observations, is there God the Father?" Dr. Jeffrey Long, medical doctor and founder of the Near-Death Experience Research Foundation, has spent more than twenty years building the world's largest database of near-death accounts. His team has collected more than 4,600 documented cases of people who died and returned to tell the story. Dr. Long's research includes a collection of testimonies based on multiple validated questions developed by some of the world's leading medical doctors and academics. In his book *God and the Afterlife,* Long focused exclusively on investigating hundreds of encounters people had with God during their near-death experience. Regardless whether they believed in the existence of God or not before dying, Long's extended study revealed that after the NDE there was an 86 percent increase in those who testified that "God definitely exists." NDErs often report experiencing healing, forgiveness and unconditional love in the presence of God. The large amount of data and "the overwhelming evidence from the largest near-death study in history" demonstrates that "God is real and He loves all of us unconditionally," Long concluded.

Skeptics questioned whether near-death experiences are real journeys in the afterlife or mere hallucinations of a dying brain. As I have already told you, science is built on observations, but what I found in the case of near-death studies is that skeptics haven't had these experiences themselves, but they also throw out the cumulative observations because they are inconvenient to their world view. When this happens, the conclusion can be nothing more than an opinion founded on literally nothing. When thousands upon thousands of testimonies from every corner of the world independently corroborate, they become data pointing to the truth. Dr. Long's study also revealed that 96 percent of NDErs declare with absolute certainty that "the experience [of the afterlife] is definitely real." These people visit another place of this grand reality of life, have encounters that completely transform the way of living, and then return to tell us their story."

3.

"This is the most precious thing in my life," said Mary and picked up a beige notepad from under the pile of papers on her desk. On its cover was scribbled in pencil *Personal encounters with Jesus Christ."*

"Jesus told his disciples," she continued, "In My Father's house there are many rooms. And if I go and prepare a place for you, I will come back and welcome you into My presence, so that you also may be where I am." To the criminal dying on the cross, Jesus said "Truly I tell you, today you will be with me in paradise." Therefore, my third question was, "according to the data, is Jesus Christ alive in the afterlife? Is Jesus with God in heaven?"

"There are countless testimonies out there, but I have written down only about 120 accounts of people who met Jesus Christ in the afterlife, and then documented their cases in scientific databases. These data not only demonstrate that Jesus is real and alive, but also reveal several things about him," she said.

Mary carefully opened the notepad and started reading.

"These are the very words of people like you and me who met Jesus face to face."

1. Jesus Christ is real

This is from a woman who died in a car accident: "I saw Jesus. He just walked by me and when he touched me, he just breathed life into me. Jesus is real."

William says, "It was real. I knew it was Jesus, and I can never deny it."

"Everything went black and then I saw a bright light. In the light, I saw Jesus sitting in a chair. He just looked at me and smiled. He looked just as I thought he would, with the white robe and glowing light all around him. The experience gave me validation that Jesus does exist" - Caren

Sharon testifies that "Jesus walked up to me. Jesus had a smile that melted my heart. He told me he loved me, that he had walked beside me every day of my life. I just stared at him. I was speechless, as he stood there declaring his love for me. I met and spoke with Jesus."

"I know there is a love that transcends all others, that Jesus is who he says he is and he loves me. My past flashed before me, out of my control. I learned that we are meant to live in love and harmony. God is the source of all love and Jesus is who he says he is." - Victor

Another woman named Susan says that "I was suddenly aware of the most heavenly light that was all-encompassing. I was in the presence of a divine being, one called the Son of God, Jesus."

"Before [my death] I was questioning if God was real. During and after the NDE, I knew God and Jesus Christ were real and felt bad for questioning my beliefs. My life changed forever at that point. I knew that there was life after death and that Jesus Christ was real." - Johnny

Odell recalls, "Standing before me was Jesus in all his glory. Jesus stretched his hand toward me and immediately all my guilt fell away and I received the most overpowering feeling of love from him. I now know God and Jesus are real. I know Jesus is real because I've seen him. I have touched him. I have talked to him. I have held his hand. I have felt his love."

"Jesus is more beautiful, wonderful and glorious than I can explain. His face was as if it were liquid crystal glass made up of pure love, light and life. His face had the colors of the rainbow and colors I cannot describe inside it. They came out and off him as the waves of the ocean coming on to the shore. I was seeing Jesus and I was a part of Jesus. I was in Jesus and Jesus was shining out of me. All of it was life. I just wanted to praise him forever." - Dean

"But not all who experience an NDE encounter Jesus Christ," I said. "Why is that?"

"Do all people who go to London personally meet the queen? Or do all who travel to Washington meet the president of the United States? Jesus is the one who decides to meet NDErs, not they."

2. People instantly know Jesus Christ

Derry says, "His countenance shone forth with such a brightness that I can't describe. I knew this heavenly personage was Jesus. He didn't announce who he was because it wasn't necessary."

Mark notes, "There was Jesus Christ. His eyes were like flames of black fire. I was looking into another universe without limits, endless in size and made of the pure substance of love. I knew that I knew that I knew I had just been face to face with Jesus Christ himself."

"I knew he was Jesus Christ. I don't know how I knew this, but I knew that he knew me more than I knew myself." says Howard. People who stand before Jesus instantly know Him.

"God exists, no doubt about it. I saw Jesus Christ with my own eyes and the light was beyond supreme, beyond glorious and beyond perfect. I felt unworthy to even look at him." - Edward

Genny recalls, "I knew immediately it was Jesus Christ himself! He looked very kind, loving and fairly young. Jesus was calling my name."

"I knew I was with Jesus," says Laura. "Though I cannot tell you what he looked like because there seemed to be just light, I was very aware I was in his embrace of pure love."

"I entered a room and found there Jesus Christ. He stretched out a file with some papers and started reading everything I had done [while] on earth." - Mukurarinda

"I saw Jesus," recalls Carolyn. "I instinctively knew him automatically."

"The light was so bright that nothing on earth could match it. [As] I drew closer, there was Jesus Christ. He gave me a choice to go with him now or to go back to be with my family." - Ron

"I discovered that my girlfriend was cheating on me, so I washed down several bottles of drugs with a bottle of rum" confesses Jeffrey. "As I looked up…Jesus had a look of disappointment on his face that touched me to my soul and made me feel so ashamed."

Seth remembers, "It was Jesus, I just knew it, even though he didn't say my name, I didn't ask his either. It was like we always knew each other and he loved me so much! Jesus is still alive."

"I looked around and noticed a white figure to my left side. There was no mistaking who this figure was. It was my Lord Jesus." - Barbara

3. Jesus Christ knows everything about you

"Something inside of me said "Stand up! You are in the presence of *the* Son of God," remembers George. Jesus "knows every single minute detail of your life. You can't think one thing and speak another. There's no hypocrisy in that place."

"Everything that I was, had done, had thought, I knew Jesus knew it all." - Howard

"I turned to my right and looked straight into the eyes of Jesus," recalls Linda. "They were dark and so full of love. I knew he knew everything about me inside out. I knew he instantly knew every thought I'd ever had, every act I had ever done, everything, totally everything about me."

Gary says, "It was Jesus Christ. The first second I saw him I knew he knew everything about me, my past, my present, my future. I could feel and sense there was nothing I could say to this being that he didn't already know. I felt bad because I could feel him in my head and I could feel I couldn't deceive him in any way."

Dr. Richard Eby remembers, "I was dead on impact. Instantly, I arrived at a place that was so ecstatically loaded with love. I knew it was heaven. The first time I heard the Lord's voice, he said, "Dick, you're dead!" Though I heard the voice within me. I asked, "Why did you call me Dick?" (only family and intimate friends called him Dick). Jesus replied, "When I died for you on the cross, it was a most intimate thing."

Another woman confessed, "I recognized [him] as Jesus Christ. I looked into his eyes. They were piercing but loving. When he looked at you, he looked straight through you and into you. You realized immediately that he knew all there was to know about you."

Carlie Terradez died of a severe asthma attack when she was 14 years old. She left her body and floated towards a bright light when was stopped before some impressive golden gates. A being radiating love appeared in front of her, put his finger under her chin, lifted her head and told her "it is not your time." She instantly knew that "Jesus knew me. He knew everything about me."

4. Jesus Christ loves you unconditionally

"NDErs report waves of love flowing into them when they meet Jesus Christ," continued Mary.

Joe remembers his near-death experience. "Who are you?" I said. He replied "I am your Lord Jesus." I fell to my knees. "Don't be afraid," he said, "I love you." I don't have the words to express the feeling of his presence. He had unconditional love towards me."

"I was sitting at a plain wooden table," Bella recalls, "Jesus sat next to me. I remember feeling a sense of total love. There was no judgment, only pure love. I was face to face with Jesus."

"Jesus said to me, "I have so much love for my babies." I could feel all his feelings of love — waves of love, of energy, of power," remembers Yvonne.

Ian walked into the light and "there was Jesus with pure white robes and arms wide stretched. Looking into his face was like looking to eternity within eternity. Waves after waves of love."

"There was a man standing before me and I immediately knew he was Jesus. I felt like I was the most precious, most loved, most beloved person in existence" says Julie.

"I looked in the smiling face of a man who said his name was Jesus," remembers Marylin. His voice was very soft and kind, almost musical. I felt pure love, complete safety and trust."

John says "I will never forget the radiation of his love as he stood near me. It was the most perfect love I have ever felt."

"When I looked into Jesus' eyes, they were like flames of fire changing colors of red, orange, blue, green, yellow and many others. In his eyes I saw the love for every human and creation of God. At first it seemed as if his eyes had love only for me, but when I thought about someone else, I saw his love for that person." - Dean

Sonya observed that "Jesus uses very few words. His eyes ooze with love. During the ordeal, I was talking to Jesus and I wasn't aware of my physical body being stabbed."

"There was love all around me, much more love than a person can feel here on earth. I fell to my knees. I couldn't look up. I knew it was Jesus. I was in the presence of the Lord." - Teresa

Alexa remembers "everything in that setting was gone, except the heavenly crowd and Jesus Christ. He gazed at me with incredible love. He loved and accepted me totally."

"Jesus Christ was seated next to God. I stood there in absolute awe at the beauty of Jesus. Jesus was wearing a white robe with a purple sash and had flames in his eyes." - Erica

Mark confesses that "The glory I saw within Jesus was endless, with no boundaries. Looking into his eyes was like looking into an endless universe of pure love."

"The radiance and light of Christ was blasting through. His radiance and his love overpowered me. He looked at me with nothing but love" says Ryan.

"When he looked at me, his eyes pierced me, they went all the way through me. Just pure love! I melted in his presence. [Jesus's] eyes were deep, beautiful pools of love and they were blue. I have since learned that Jews from the tribe of Judah are known to have blue eyes." - Gary

"Jesus Christ himself reached down and picked me up," Theresa recalls. "I felt so undeserving. Jesus held me, I looked into his eyes and I will never forget how wonderful his eyes were. The first thing I said to him was, do you hate me because I'm a drug addict? I will never forget what he said to me: "No. I only want you to know that I love you.""

"I saw Jesus at the center of the light. Love poured out upon me, like warm water. When I saw Jesus, it was as if every piece of the puzzle from my life fell into place. I felt validated." - Jean

"I saw my body when the doctor was working on me. [Then] I saw Mama Mary and I saw Jesus Christ. Jesus Christ was on his throne. He had very brilliant white clothes." - Juan

Nathan was in clinical death for 26 minutes without a heartbeat. He recalls, "I saw a bright light and I saw Jesus. He reached out and grabbed my hand. He told me, "Don't be afraid." I was at peace the whole time. I could clearly see him."

Phillip's heart stopped beating and his brain activity was 0.00%. He was clinically dead for 4 hours. "I was released from the dark tunnel into pure light. I saw a figure approach [me], and the moment I saw him I knew it was Jesus the Christ. There was an irrepressible feeling of love."

Lisa suffered a heart attack on Christmas day. She was shocked seventeen times during resuscitation. She says, "I truly believed he was Jesus Christ. He showed more love than I ever experienced. To be looked at with so much love, there are no big enough words."

"Jesus greeted me with such unconditional love," says Kim. "There was no shame, no blame and no condemnation towards me. Only pure, unconditional love. He asked me to give him my pain and he said this was the reason why he was born into the world. He lives."

"I felt neither condemnation nor shame. At first I hardly dared to look at Jesus, but after a time I felt my body being lifted up. Then I was standing before him. As he smiled at me, relief poured over my soul. "Welcome home, Samaa," he said in a voice sweet and gentle, yet also powerful, like the sound of many waters. He opened his arms to me. His beautiful eyes were like blazing fires of consuming love that overwhelmed me."

5. Jesus Christ still has the crucifixion marks in his body in the afterlife

"I felt no fear at all" Linda declares. "Just the strongest love I have ever felt from anyone anywhere in my entire existence. When I was almost close enough to touch him, [Jesus] lifted his hands like a stop sign. I could see the scars in his hands - or his wrists I should say."

Micki remembers, "I turned to my left and there stood Jesus Christ. I could see his nail prints in his hands and feet. But they were not in his palms, they were more in his wrist area and angled out as though they were torn from his weight."

"I fell to my face" says Brent. "I could not stand, the light was all powerful. I heard his voice say, 'Open your eyes.' The moment I opened my eyes, I saw feet, and holes in these feet. As he reached out his hand, I saw nail prints - not in his palm or forearms - but in his wrists. I grabbed his hand and I was able to stand up. I felt this unexplainable intense love. I knew it was Jesus."

"My first question was, "How do I know you are Jesus?" He held out his hands. I saw a pair of pure white hands, except for a light red streak mark towards the palm wrist area." - Kathaleen

Standing before Jesus, Gary noticed "where nails had been driven into his hands, not his palms as some paintings depict, but into his wrists." Mary lifted her eyes from the notepad and smiled. "Do you know that medical doctors that actually studied the crucifixion corroborate with what NDErs testify about the position of the nail marks being in his wrists?"

She then resumed reading.

"[Jesus] held out his hands in front of me and I saw the nail scars. The wounds were open, shining with a beautiful light." - Richard

"Jesus has markers. He had colors on him," four-year old Colton told his father when he woke up after surgery. When asked what color, Colton answered, "Red, daddy. Jesus has red markers on him." His father then asked Colton where Jesus's markers were, and the boy pointed to both hands and the tops of his feet. "That's where Jesus' markers are," he said.

6. Jesus Christ is real regardless of what people believe prior to their NDE

"I was looking down at my body and I was aware of a presence sort of to my right and behind me. I realized Jesus was there. It surprised me as I was agnostic," says Lisa.

"I was in Jesus's presence, [and] I felt nothing but pure bliss. I wasn't entirely convinced Jesus really existed as a human on earth, [but] this experience obliterated any doubts." - Eric

"Everything around [me] was dark. Then I saw the figure of a man who stood over a sort of stream. All was dazzling in him. He seemed to be made of light. I felt extremely good in his presence. Full of unconditional, absolute love. I knew he was Jesus Christ who I didn't believe in. I was surprised and said "but you don't exist…!" He replied "Live," but I didn't want to return. I knew when I was before him that he was Jesus Christ who I didn't believe in." - Irene

"I became aware that the God I was experiencing was not just a life force or some impersonal consciousness, but God had a personality," says John. "God had a sense of humor. We laughed at the thought of me questioning His existence. I realized I was the shadow and He was the reality."

"I am Jewish and I do not believe in Jesus Christ. I only believe in God," a woman says. She was involved with her husband and children in a car accident and found herself out of her body, viewing the scene from above. "[A] hand touched mine and I turned to see and there was Jesus Christ. I never wanted to leave this man, I wanted to stay with [Jesus] and hold his hand."

"Jesus had the angels sing to me because I was so scared" says four-year-old Colton. "They made me feel better. I was sitting in Jesus' lap."

7. Jesus Christ saves people from hell

"Mainstream books as well as scientific articles don't usually report frightening NDEs because they are very disturbing to the people who experience them," said Mary. "Many don't want to even think, remember or talk about them at all. Nonetheless, they are real. Investigating the archives of several scientific projects, I discovered the following testimonies."

"God was not pleased with my life of alcohol and drugs. I was shown a place of intense horror. Just before being consumed, I was guided away by a person I knew to be Christ Jesus." - Bruce

This account was written by a relative of a man, previously addicted to heroin and still an alcoholic, who died in a car crash. He recalls finding himself on the verge of falling into a dark pit, with a multitude of creatures chasing him to drag him into deeper darkness. His family members, who were not sure whether this man had ever heard of Jesus Christ before, wrote down his testimony. "The faces of these beings were tortured with anguish and fury. They were frightening. This was the most frightening experience he ever had in his life. What was this place exactly like? "A place of misfortune," he testifies. A hand held back this man while he was on the verge of falling down into the pit. He recalls being saved by "the One nailed on the cross."

Howard Storm testifies, "we were anti-Christian. It was cool if people explored exotic spiritualities, but the Christian tradition was treated with hostility. I was an atheist and we imposed that world view on our students at the university. I knew with 100 percent certainty that when you die, it's game over. I went on a trip to Paris and ended up in the emergency room with a fatal stomach condition. Then, I died. I found myself in a dark hallway with evil beings hitting me, biting me. People are incapable to understand what these beings do to demean, humiliate and degrade you. It is a world of torment, of utter hopelessness. I was destroyed, I was gore. I heard a voice within me saying "Pray to God" and thought to myself "what a stupid idea, I don't believe in God." I didn't know any prayer, but I remembered the song *Jesus Loves Me* from when I was eleven years old. I yelled out in that darkness, "Jesus, please save me!" A light then appeared in the darkness, unbelievably bright. These arms picked me and brought me into this light, which was Jesus Christ and he filled me with his love."

"Not many people believe in hell these days," I interrupted Mary from reading.

"For you to have knowledge of something, you must either have the experience yourself or analyze the data and draw the conclusions," she said. "But to say you don't believe when you actually know nothing, it means nothing. Do you know that according to scientific research, about a quarter of NDErs report finding themselves in a place of utter darkness, hopelessness and terror, surrounded by beings screaming and howling, and dragging them in hatred towards a fiery pit? *The Handbook of Near-Death Experiences* reports that twelve different studies involving 1,369 subjects revealed that 23 percent of NDErs reported experiences "ranging from disturbing to terrifying or despairing." Dr. Pim van Lommel writes, "a terrifying NDE usually produces long-lasting emotional trauma." The exact number of people who experience hellish NDEs, often known as a "hell experience," is unknown, because shame and guilt prevent them from sharing these terrifying accounts. Dr. Penny Sartori, a leading authority on near-death experiences, noted that "negative NDEs are just as real as the pleasant ones." In 2008, researchers performed one of the largest NDE study in the Western medical world. Investigating 2060 survivors from 15 hospitals, experts found that 46 percent of NDErs reported fearful and persecutory experiences. "Not all death experiences are good," writes Dr. Maurice Rawling, "the unpleasant experiences in my study have turned out to be at least as frequent as the pleasant ones." Materialist scientists don't seem to believe this is a serious field of inquiry, but people who had these experiences aren't at all interested in what the skeptical science says. Following their NDE, 91 percent of people confessed having a wakeup call to reality and changing their beliefs and attitudes about life."

8. Jesus Christ knows your dead relatives

"This discovery brought me much comfort" said Mary and continued reading from her notebook.

"I was transported very fast through a tunnel. I was in front of Jesus Christ and behind him were my deceased father and grandmother in the clothes we buried them in," says Henrietta.

"I went to heaven. Next thing I knew, I was staring at my grandma - my mother's mother. Behind her was her mother - my great grandmother. On the right hand side was my uncle Stanley and on the left were three of my great aunts and my cousin Will who got killed in a car wreck in 1986 when he was just 17. My grandmother, aunts and uncle were all in their eighties when they died, but when I got to heaven, they were all in their mid thirties. They were so young and beautiful. Behind them, was standing Jesus Christ himself. He held his hands out and showed me the holes in his hands. He said "I am your Christ." I didn't know what to do. I was in awe," Cecil recalls.

Dean says, "On the other side of Jesus was my family. My grandmother Mary and with her, other relatives. Generation after generation after generation, of those who have accepted Jesus Christ as Lord and Savior, that produced me on this planet. They came to greet me."

"In the garden were two people," Lariza remembers. "One wore a white tunic, it was Jesus Christ, and beside him was my brother who died in a car accident when I was eight years old. My brother asked me, "What are you doing here?" Jesus told me, "Go back. It is not your time.""

"My grandmother, deceased for years, was present along with a beaming light I recognized as Jesus. "It is not your time yet. You have other lives to touch. Go back home!" he said. This light, which I recognized as Jesus, had the power to give me life. He was in control, not I" - Sebastian

Cathy says, "I saw Jesus holding my five year old son who had died two years earlier in an accident. They were both dressed in white, standing or floating in this bright light. I couldn't see much of anything else, I was too focused on seeing my son. Jesus was holding him. Jesus put him down and he came to me, I was so happy to see him. Now I don't just believe in God and Jesus Christ and heaven, I know it's there!"

"I saw my sister who had passed away twenty-one years before my [NDE]," says Linda. "She greeted me and told me there was someone she wanted me to meet. Jesus Christ came and there was no mistake as to who he was. He looked me straight in the eyes and said, "I have come for you that you may know that I am real.""

"Jesus was holding me like a child. I felt a rush of overwhelming love and joy flooding me in a warm, honey-like texture. He didn't actually identify himself, but I knew him. My grandparents, who died in 2003 and 2006 were at the foot of my bed. There is no doubt in my mind, I was with Jesus."- Jill

Chris recalls, "I saw both of my grandmothers. They hugged me and my dad's mom took my hand and said she had someone she wanted me to meet. I saw a man with long white hair and robe with gold trim playing with children. He arose and walked towards us. When he reached us, my grandma said, "Honey, this is your Lord and Savior, Jesus Christ." He touched my forehead with two fingers of his left hand and said, "It's not your time. You cannot stay.""

"Jesus appeared in front of me and I could do nothing but fall to my knees. Then Jesus said, "You are worthy child, rise." So I did and faced the Lord Jesus Christ with utmost guilt and feelings of insignificance. Jesus said, "You have learned from your mistakes, my child. You will return and you will show others the way. You will spread the love of God." At this moment, I was in the presence of my deceased relatives, two uncles, an aunt, a grandfather and a great-grandmother. None spoke but they pointed to the 'ground', indicating [that] I must return," remembers Jed.

In 1997, Julie, Andy and their eight-year old son Landon were involved in a devastating car wreck. Andy died instantly. Julie recovered, but Landon had suffered massive head injuries and remained in a coma for two weeks. When he finally opened his eyes, Julie decided she had to tell the boy about his father, but she didn't found the heart to break the news to him. Instead, she asked him, "Landon, do you know where your dad is?" The eight-year-old boy answered, "Yes, I know where he is. I saw him in heaven." Landon continues, "I remember being able to see my dad and his friend Owen Palmer who had passed away less than a month before he did, also in a car accident, and Owen's son Neil Palmer who had died years before." Landon then told his mother that he saw her other two kids in heaven. Julie had had two miscarriages before Landon was born, but they never disclosed this to him. "I knew they were my siblings although nobody told me about them," Landon recalls. He then met Jesus. "Jesus came to me and told me I have to go back to earth, and tell others about him."

Mary closed her notepad and carefully put it back on the desk. She took off her eye glasses and wiped a tear from her eye. "Thousands of people have returned from the afterlife and documented their testimony in scientific environments. The data is publicly available for anyone who has eyes to see and ears to hear. I miss my daughter every day, but I know that even though she came through me, she doesn't belong to me. She belongs to Jesus Christ. I know that my baby is in heaven, not because I put my hope in a fairytale, but because science confirms that Jesus Christ is more real than anything else. He is alive, and as Luke wrote in *The Book of Acts*, he "must remain in heaven" until God decides is time for him to return for us who believe.

CHAPTER 6
Behold The Son

Q6 - Does Jesus Christ appear to people today?

*"Humankind cannot bear
very much reality" - T.S. Eliot*

1.

The New Testament manuscripts describe several accounts of Jesus Christ appearing alive in bodily form to his disciples as well as to his persecutors immediately after his death. *The Gospels of Matthew* and *Mark* describe the following appearances of Jesus three days after his burial.

"Mary Magdalene, Mary the mother of James and Salome bought spices so that they might go to anoint Jesus' body. Very early on the first day of the week, just after sunrise, they were on their way to the tomb and they asked each other, "Who will roll the stone away from the entrance of the tomb?" When they looked up, however, they saw the stone, which was very large, had been rolled away. As they entered the tomb, they saw a young man dressed in a white robe sitting on the right side and they were alarmed. "Do not be afraid," he said. "You are looking for Jesus the Nazarene, who was crucified. He has risen! He is not here. See the place where they laid him. Go and tell his disciples and to Peter. He is going ahead of you into Galilee. There you will see him, just as he told you." Trembling and bewildered, the women went out and fled from the tomb. They said nothing to anyone, because they were afraid. Suddenly Jesus met them. "Greetings," he said. They came to him, clasped his feet and worshiped him. Then Jesus said to them, "Do not be afraid. Go and tell my brothers to go to Galilee. There they will see me."

The Gospel of John recounts that Jesus also appeared to Mary Magdalene after his crucifixion. Mary then went and told the disciples who were mourning and weeping, but when they learned from her that Jesus was alive and she had seen him, they didn't believe. "Later Jesus appeared to the eleven disciples as they were eating. He rebuked them for their lack of faith and their stubborn refusal to believe those who had seen him after he had risen."

The Gospel of Luke documents the risen Jesus appearing to ten of his disciples as they were hiding inside the house with the doors locked, fearing they will also be executed by the Romans. "Jesus himself stood among them and said "Peace be with you." But they were startled and frightened, and supposed they saw a ghost. Jesus said to them, "Why are you troubled and why do questionings arise in your hearts? See my hands and my feet, that it is I myself. Handle me and see, for a spirit has not flesh and bones, as you see that I have." When he said this, Jesus showed them his hands and his feet. While they still disbelieved and wondered, he said to them: "Have you anything here to eat?" They gave him a piece of broiled fish, and he took it and ate before them." Jesus appeared again to the eleven disciples a week later, the following Sunday.

In *The Book of Acts,* Luke writes that "Jesus presented himself alive after his passion by many proofs, appearing to them during forty days and speaking of the kingdom of God." Another documented appearance is attributed to Stephen. While he was being murdered by the crowd, "Stephen gazed into heaven and saw the glory of God and Jesus standing at the right hand of God." Luke also describes the appearance of Jesus to Saul. "Meanwhile, Saul was still breathing out murderous threats against the Lord's disciples. He went to the high priest and asked him for letters to the synagogues in Damascus, so that if he found any there who [were followers of Jesus], whether men or women, he might take them as prisoners to Jerusalem. As he neared Damascus on his journey, suddenly a light from heaven flashed around him. He fell to the ground and heard a voice say to him, "Saul, Saul, why do you persecute me?"
"Who are you, Lord?" Saul asked.
"I am Jesus, whom you are persecuting," he replied.
"Now get up and go into the city, and you will be told what you must do."

In *The Epistle to Corinthians*, Paul documents several appearances of Jesus after his death. He writes, "[Jesus] appeared to Cephas and then to the twelve. After that, he appeared to more than five hundred of the brothers and sisters at the same time, most of whom are still living, though some have fallen asleep. Then he appeared to James, then to all the apostles, and last of all he appeared to me also. For I am the least of the apostles…because I persecuted the church of God."

In *The Book of Acts,* Luke documents Jesus Christ appearing several times to apostle Paul. One night, Jesus appeared to him while he was in the city of Corinth in Greece, saying, "Do not be afraid. Keep on speaking. Do not be silent. For I am with you and no one will lay a hand on you because I have many people in this city." Another time, when Paul was in Jerusalem "the dispute grew so violent that the commander was afraid [the crowd] would tear Paul to pieces. He ordered the soldiers to go down and remove him by force and bring [Paul] into the barracks. The following night, the Lord [Jesus] stood by Paul and said, "Take courage! As you have testified about me in Jerusalem, so also you must testify in Rome."

Historians agree based on the wealth of available evidence that the followers of Christ believed and proclaimed that they saw Jesus alive after his crucifixion. Scholars cannot directly demonstrate that Jesus Christ was raised from the dead, but concur that his disciples at least believed they saw him again after his death in bodily form. Even skeptical scholar Dr. Bart Ehrman says that historians, of course, have no difficulty whatsoever speaking about the belief in Jesus' resurrection, since this is a matter of public record. For it is a historical fact that some of Jesus' followers came to believe that he had been raised from the dead soon after his execution. Scholars say with complete certainty that some of his disciples insisted that Jesus soon appeared to them, convincing them that he had been raised from the dead. The majority of critical scholars from leading universities around the world agree that these are historical facts backed by accurate evidence: Jesus died by crucifixion. He was buried. His death threw his disciples into grief and despair. His disciples had experiences they believed were literal bodily appearances of Jesus Christ raised from the dead. His followers were convinced that Jesus appeared to them. The experience transformed them from frightened doubters into bold proclaimers of his resurrection.

Even some of the worst enemies of early Christianity were transformed by Jesus appearing to them. Saul was converted from a violent persecutor of Christians into a great evangelist by an experience in which he believed he had met the risen Jesus. "With these data," writes professor Gary Habermas of Liberty University, "we have enough of a basis to say that Jesus died and he was actually seen again afterwards."

The New Testament reports that the appearances of the risen Jesus occurred to diverse groups of people - three women, two, ten and eleven disciples, and five hundred men among others. Critics may dismiss the appearances of the risen Christ as hallucinatory phenomena, but hallucinations do not occur to multiple individuals at once. Five hundred people cannot hallucinate the same person at the same moment in time. "Within these groups of people," says Habermas, "many different personality types as well as both genders were represented, from hardheaded Peter, to tenderhearted John, to (presumably) the softhearted Marys, along with all of the others. The different genders, personalities, times and places involved all lengthen the odds against hallucinations. It's highly unlikely that, among those different groups, each of these people would be precisely in just the proper frame of mind to see [the same] hallucination."

The disciples were instantly transformed by Jesus' appearances to the point that they were willing to be executed than deny that Jesus had risen from the dead. The resurrection of Christ is "of first importance" and the one fact that early followers were certain of. In fact, the bodily resurrection of Jesus is the central focus of Christianity and, as the first apostles themselves declared, "if Christ had not been raised, then our preaching is vain and your faith also is vain."

The disciples didn't say that after his death "Jesus lives in our hearts," or that "the spirit of Jesus Christ went to heaven," that "his memory will remain with us forever," or that they've seen Jesus as a ghost or as a luminous body. His followers clearly declared the resurrection of Jesus Christ in bodily form. However, Jesus didn't rise from the dead to live an ordinary existence. He was not resuscitated and did not return from the dead as those whom he himself had raised from the dead. Those whom he had brought back from the dead, though they live, will die again. Jesus Christ was resurrected to an eternal life in a glorified body. He will never die again. This glorified body made of flesh and bones still bares the wounds of the cross, and also has new and extraordinary qualities. "The resurrected Jesus has a transformed body. In his resurrected body, Jesus can veil his presence and appear when and how he wills," says Dr. Brant Pitre of The Augustine Institute. "The risen Jesus has not discarded his human body like an old garment. The crucifixion has literally left his marks on him forever." In his glorified body, Jesus can appear and disappear at will, he can move from the spiritual to the physical, and from the invisible to the visible dimensions. When the disciples proclaim that Jesus had risen from the dead, they do not mean he was restored to an earthly life, but rather that he was resurrected to the eternal life.

The Gospel of Luke recalls the following account. "Two of Jesus's followers were walking to the village of Emmaus, seven miles from Jerusalem. As they walked along, Jesus himself suddenly came and began walking with them. But God kept them from recognizing him…By this time they were nearing Emmaus and the end of their journey. Jesus acted as if he were going on but they begged him, "stay with us since it's getting late. So he went home with them. As they sat down to eat, he took the bread and blessed it. Then he broke it and gave it to them. Suddenly, their eyes were opened and they recognized him. And at that moment he disappeared!"

Dr. Ben Witherington III, professor of New Testament at Asbury Theological Seminary, observed that the gospel writers did not say "I *saw* Jesus," but rather testified that "Jesus *appeared* and spoke" to them. His presence was never something initiated by people. This is especially true in the case of those who persecuted the early disciples. Jesus himself took the initiative to appear to them according to his own will and disappeared once he had delivered his message. If Jesus appeared alive to his disciples and to his enemies days, months and even years after his death as the gospels declare, the fair question to ask is does Jesus Christ appear to people today?

2.

Several sources outside the Bible describing ancient and medieval encounters with Jesus Christ include *A Dictionary of Miracles* by E.C. Brewer and *The Apparitions and Shrines of Heaven's Queen* by W.J. Walsh. These books document thousands of entries of different kinds of miraculous events.

In year 41 AD, Jesus Christ appeared to his mother Mary at the hour of her death. Several disciples were with her during the last moments of her life, when the house was filled with a heavenly fragrance and "Jesus himself appeared, accompanied by a brilliant cortege of angels and saints, and the soul of Mary, leaving her mortal tenement, ascended with her son to heaven."

Martha, the sister of Mary and Lazarus whom Jesus raised from the dead, had been exiled in Marseilles, France. One night in year 84 AD, Jesus appeared to her. "Here am I, Martha," he said. "As you served me with so much devotion and showed me such hospitality in Bethany, I am now come to redeem you from exile, that where I am you may be also. Farewell Martha, for a little time. I go and prepare a place for you." In the morning, Martha breathed her last. In the same time, on the other side of town, the local bishop was alone in the church when Jesus appeared to him and said, "My son, come with me to celebrate Martha's funeral." The bishop went with Jesus. When the funeral was over and everyone left, one of the church workers asked Jesus who he was and where he came from. Jesus didn't answer, but gave him a book he had in his hands. The worker opened the book and read on every page the words, "The memory of Martha, the hostess of Jesus, will be everlasting."

In year 320 AD, Jesus appeared to forty soldiers from different countries who were about to be executed for their faith in Christ. They refused to dishonor Jesus by sacrificing to pagan idols and had been thrown in prison. In the night, Jesus Christ appeared to them during prayer and said: "He that believed in me, though he dies yet he shall live, and whosoever liveth and believed in me shall never die. Fear not them that can torment the body only, but know this. To him that overcomes will I give to eat of the tree of life which is in the midst of the paradise of God."

Martin of Tours, who lived between 336 and 397 AD, was serving in the Roman army during a severe winter. One day, when many people perished from the cold, Martin was marching through the city with his regiment. They came upon a beggar trembling naked on the ground. Martin removed his military cloak, cut it in two with his sword, and gave half to the beggar and the other half he threw over his shoulders as a scarf. Some of his companions laughed at him, while others were ashamed for having done nothing for this man. In the night, Jesus Christ appeared to Martin wearing the parted cloak, saying "What is done to the poor in my name is done unto me."

In 494 AD, a priest of Mount Preclaro in Italy was about to eat his dinner when Jesus appeared to him, saying "A servant of mine is dying of hunger in a cavern, while you are to indulge yourself on these dainties." The priest rose at once, took the food with him and went to this cavern, some fifty miles away from Rome. He found the man there and they ate together.

Several accounts describe people giving gifts to the poor and finding Jesus Christ to be the recipient. One of the earliest accounts is that of Gregory the Great, 540 - 604 AD, who regularly gave to the poor. One night after Gregory fed the beggars, Jesus appeared to him and said, "Ordinarily you receive me in the poor that assemble at your board, but today you received me personally."

In 619 AD, a man by the name of Peter was a banker and governor in Africa. One day he gave his coat to a naked beggar, but the man immediately sold the coat. Peter was angered by the gesture, but on his way home, Jesus Christ appeared to him dressed in the garment he had just given away. "Peter, what you give to the poor in my name you give unto me," Jesus said to him. "Seek neither gratitude nor glory in this world, your reward is in the world to come." Peter then left everything to become a follower of Christ.

In 714 AD, a young man from Brittany by the name of Hubert was ordained priest at only 20 years old. During the dinner ceremony, a beggar sat himself at the table together with the high and honored guests. Hubert placed the food before him, but the man vanished. The nobles immediately knew that the beggar was Jesus Christ.

In 983 AD, Wulsin of Dorsetshire was moments away from death when he whispered to those gathered around him: "I see the heavens open and Jesus standing at the right hand of God."

In 1014 AD, Henry, the duke of Bavaria, traveled to Rome to be enthroned Emperor. Henry's custom on arriving in another town was to spend his first night in prayer. On the night of his arrival in Rome, Henry was praying in St. Mary Major cathedral when he "saw the sovereign and eternal priest Christ Jesus" enter together with saints and angels singing in his presence.

In 1109 AD, a student from the city of Lyons by the name of Robert asked God to show him the way into heaven. One day he had a vision of a vast land and a magnificent city on top of a high mountain. Robert wanted to enter, but found it impossible to cross the river flowing between him and the city. He noticed several men washing their garments in the water and another man dressed in a shinning robe of dazzling white standing by them. "Who are you?" asked Robert. "These poor ones" the man replied, "are monks washing away their sins by repentance and making their robes white in the river of tears. I am Jesus Christ, ever ready to help the truly penitent. The city you see is paradise where I reign with those who have washed their robes and made them white. Behold, the road to heaven which you wanted to see."

Julián of Cuenca, 1127 - 1208 AD, had the custom of offering meals to several paupers each day. On one occasion, a man "clad in mean apparel, but not having a mean demeanor" came to eat supper. Julian took him aside after the meal and asked the man where was he coming from. The pauper replied, "My dear Julian, I thank you for your hospitality to the poor and I promise you eternal life. Be well assured that whatever you do to the least of these my brethren, you do unto me." Julián immediately knew the man was Jesus Christ.

One night while he was praying, Dominic of Osma, 1170 - 1221 AD, saw Jesus Christ sitting on a throne enveloped in glory. Jesus was angry for the sins and the iniquity of people. Dominic also observed that nobody from the heavenly crowd dared to oppose God's anger with their prayers.

In 1220 AD, Hyacinth of Kiev was attending church one day when he suddenly saw a dazzling light descending from heaven and a procession of angels in the midst of it. He then witnessed Jesus crowning his mother Mary with a crown of flowers and stars. Mary then took it from her head and said, "Behold, [Hyacinth]! This crown is for you."

In 1221 AD, Francis of Assisi was in church in Italy one day when he saw Jesus accompanied by his mother Mary and a multitude of angels. They appeared to Francis to encourage him to "ask a favor for salvation of souls." Jesus appeared again to Francis in 1223 and gave him three white and three red roses of exquisite beauty as material evidence of the reality of his vision. This took place in the dead of winter when no rose was anywhere to be found.

Jesus appeared to Rosa of Viterbo, 1233 – 1251 AD, suspended on the cross, his hands and feet nailed, his head pierced with thorns, his face black and blue, his limbs dislocated, the flesh torn off his bones, and his body covered with blood. Rosa screamed, shuddered and fainted. When she came to herself, she was unable to speak, but only looked upon Jesus before her. She cried out "O my Jesus, why are thou reduced to this pitiable state? What inhuman monsters could have used thee thus?" Jesus answered, "this [is] my love, my burning love for man."

Lutgardis of Aywières was brought up in a convent in the territory that is now Belgium in Europe. Though she was raised in the monastery, she had no interest in Christianity. One night in 1246 AD, Jesus Christ appeared to her in person saying, "Lutgardis, how ought you not to love me? Leave the vanities of the world and you shall find in me the delights of divine love." These words changed her life in an instant and ever since she followed the One who appeared to her.

Mechtilde of Hackeborn saw Jesus with many angels in 1293 AD. Her sister Gertrude saw Jesus in 1334 AD. Mechtilde reported Jesus telling her, "In the morning, let your first act be to greet my heart and to offer me your own. Whoever breathes a sigh toward me draws me to himself." In another vision, Jesus himself recommended the Bible. Opening to her the wound of his heart, Jesus said to Mechtilde: "Consider how great is my love. If you want to know it well, you will not find it expressed more clearly anywhere than in the gospels. No one has ever expressed stronger or more tender feelings than these. As my Father has loved me, so have I loved you."

Angela of Foligno spoke just before her death in 1309 AD: "Christ, the Son of God, had now presented me to the Father and these words were said to me: "O my bride, my beautiful one! O, thou that are loved by me with great love, I desire that you shouldn't come to me with sorrow, but with joy and with the royal robe." And [Jesus] showed me the royal robe, even as a bridegroom shows it to his bride, but it was not of purple nor of scarlet, but it was a kind of marvelous light with which the soul is clothed."

Catherine of Siena, 1317 - 1380 AD, was alone in her monastic cell when she cried out in prayer, "O Savior, give me grace that nothing may separate me from your great love!" A voice then spoke to her, "Be at peace, Catherine, I will never leave you nor forsake you." The cell was filled with light and Jesus Christ came with his angels. He placed a ring of gold with a large diamond and four precious stones around it on Catherine's finger, saying "I, thy Creator, with my Father which is in heaven, I, thy redeemer and thy spouse, will preserve thee pure, till that day when I come to claim you as my heavenly bride." On another day, a beggar asked alms of Catherine and she was distressed because she had nothing to give to him. Happening to cast her eyes on the rosary, she noticed the silver crucifix which she gave to the beggar. In the night, while she was in prayer, Jesus appeared to her holding the crucifix now studded with precious stones. "Do you recognize this crucifix, my daughter?" asked Jesus. "Yes," answered Catherine. "This morning you gave it to me in pure love. On the day of judgement I will restore it to you as you now see it" he said and vanished from her sight. Another time, Catherine saw above the church in her town a glorious throne where Jesus sat dressed in a majestic robe. Jesus fixed his eyes on her and beheld Catherine with mercy. Her brother who was with her didn't see anything.

In 1396 AD, Vincent Ferrier fell ill and every one in his family believed he was going to die. On the night of October 3, Vincent's chamber was filled with a brilliant light and Jesus Christ appeared to him saying "Vincent, rise up safe and sound, and go forth to preach against sin. For this end have I chosen thee. Warn sinners to be converted, for the kingdom of heaven is at hand." Jesus touched Vincent's face with his right hand. "O my Vincent, rise," he said and Vincent was instantly healed.

When Angela de Merici, 1474 - 1540 AD, was only twenty-two years of age, she felt in her heart the calling to establish free schools for education of girls regarding purity and virginity. She also had a vision of virgins and angels ascending to heaven on a ladder. Angela ignored both the calling and the vision, and did nothing about them. Forty nine years later, Jesus appeared to her. His face was angry, his manner menacing and he bore a whip in his hand. Jesus asked her how it was that she had neglected for nearly fifty years the work he had sent her to do. She begged for forgiveness, and immediately summoned her companions and started working on the schools.

In 1464 AD, Jesus Christ appeared to twelve-year-old Stephana Quinzani in Italy, saying, "My daughter, since for the love of me you have generously stripped of your own will, ask what you will and I will grant it to you." Stephana answered, "I desire nothing but thyself, Lord."

Jesus appeared to the mother of Columba of Rieti in 1493 AD. When Columba left home to become a nun in the monastery, her mother was greatly distressed. One day, a beggar showed up at her door and approached the crying mother: "Woman, I see your heart is very sorrowful." "How so?" she replied. "I can see it" said the stranger, "but believe me, that which has occurred has happened by the will of God. Your daughter has leaned on a staff that can never break. Be comforted for you will soon see the hand of God in this affliction." The man then disappeared. When Columba was twelve years old, Jesus Christ appeared to her seated on the throne of glory.

Ernest Clifton was a fifteen-century English monk who abandoned the monastic life to indulge in the pleasures of this world. He settled on operating an inn, where each depravity led to another. The man descended deeper and deeper into evil. He stole from travelers and ended up even murdering some of his patrons. One night he entered a room to stab the occupant, but instead of his intended victim, he found himself looking at Jesus Christ covered with the wounds of crucifixion. Jesus looked at Ernest and said, "Do you wish to kill me again? Stretch forth your hand and murder me again." Clifton was so shaken by this experience that he confessed his crimes to the authorities.

Julian of Norwich had several visions of Jesus Christ on May 13, 1373 AD. The showings, as Julian named them, took place over a few hours, when Julian was overcome with an illness that almost claimed her life. She saw Jesus on the cross and witnessed his love. After these visions, she dared to do what nobody else had done before. Julian wrote the first book ever written in the English language by a woman. The book is titled *Revelations of Divine Love*.

Jesus appeared to Teresa of Ávila, 1515 - 1582 AD, saying: "Fear not, my daughter, it is I who speak. I will never leave you nor forsake you." On another occasion, Jesus Christ appeared to her and putting his right hand into her hand, he said: "See this nail print. It is the sign of my marriage contract with you. Ere long you shall be my bride and nothing shall separate you from the love of God your Savior." Teresa cried out, "O God, enlarge my heart or it will burst with love." Years later when Teresa founded the monastery of Seville, Jesus Christ appeared to her again."You know, daughter, there is a marriage contract between you and me. You are mine and I am yours."

Agnès Galand, 1602 - 1634 AD, prayed that she might be taken from this life of tears and suffering, when Jesus appeared to her: "I want your services still to sanctify souls to my glory."

Mary Margaret Alacoque, 1648 - 1690 AD, was a nun in Burgundy, France. One day when Mary was going to communion, Jesus Christ appeared to her and put a crown on her head, saying: "My daughter, take this crown in token of that which will be given you in the Church triumphant." In

1674, Jesus appeared to her again, took his heart and put it into her chest. She saw it with her own eyes and testified that Jesus's heart was burning as iron heated in a furnace. Whenever Mary mentioned these visions to anyone, people mocked her and she didn't know what do to. Jesus appeared to her again and showed her his five wounds blazing with light. He told her of his great love for man and of man's ingratitude to him. On February 8, 1661, Jesus appeared again to Mary, saying: "Daughter, here is the heart whose love to man is so great, but from whom I receive nothing but ingratitude." Floods of fire blazed forth from his heart.

In 1903, fourteen-year-old Sundar Singh met some Christians in India who gave him a New Testament to read. In anger, Sundar burned the Bible page by page in front of his friends. Time passed and he wasn't able to find any meaning in life. Sundar resolved to kill himself. He asked that whosoever is the true God to appear before him or else he would throw himself on a railroad track. In the same night, a bright cloud filled his room and Jesus Christ appeared before him. Singh was converted and became a Christian missionary. "I am not worthy to follow in the steps of my Lord," he said, "but, like him, I want no home, no possessions. Like him, I will belong to the road, sharing the suffering of my people, eating with those who will give me shelter and telling all men of the love of God."

In one of T.L. Osborn's evangelical campaigns in India in the 1960s, somewhere in the back of the crowd there was a young student from the university. He was a fanatic member of the Arya Samaj, the Hindu movement that promotes belief in the infallible authority of the Indian scriptures the Vedas. He hated Jesus and swore to drive Christianity out from the shores of India. The young man stood with his arms folded across his chest in contempt when suddenly Jesus Christ appeared before him. He opened his arms and said "Behold, I am Jesus." The student fell in the dust crying. When he finally got a hold of himself, he ran to the platform, grabbed the microphone with trembling hands and testified to thousands of people: "Accept this Jesus. I saw him. I saw the scars in his hands. He is alive!"

Segatashya was born in July 1967 in a remote area of Rwanda in a cluster of mud huts and goat pens. The tiny rural community was not connected by roads to the rest of the country and the closest village was miles away through the African bush. Segatashya was born in a pagan family who honored the spirits of the dead relatives. They didn't know who Jesus was nor they had ever seen a Bible. On July 2, 1982, Segatashya was in the field with the goats when he heard someone calling him. "I am Jesus Christ," the voice said and instructed the boy to go to the neighbor's house and deliver a message. Segatashya obeyed. "Jesus Christ sent me here today to tell you and all men to renew your hearts," he told them. Then Jesus appeared to Segatashya. "Look up and behold the one who has been talking to you," said Jesus. The boy recalls, "I looked up and a dazzling light filled the sky. The light was brilliant and the sky was filled with a million shinning flowers. Jesus appeared in the heavens in the midst of the flowers. He was bathed in a luminous light that surrounded him and shone out from within his body." Segatashya became a messenger for Jesus Christ in Africa, preaching repentance of sins and living with a pure and perfect heart before God. When Segatashya shared with the masses the messages Jesus gave him, he was quoting the Bible in exact words even though he never had a day's education in his life and he couldn't read or write. "What you need to know," Segatashya told Immaculée Ilibagiza who documented his story, is that "Jesus knows the very depths of our souls, all our dreams and worries, all our hopes and fears, all our goodness and all our weakness. Pray with sincerity. To be near [Jesus] is to live in love, no words need to be spoken. Ask him into your heart and all his graces are yours. If you are able to know only one truth in your life, you should know this truth: Jesus loves you." Jesus Christ appeared to Segatashya several times during his short life.

3.

Testimonies from ancient past may not be considered adequate by modern science, and therefore contemporary evidence is required to further investigate the reality of these accounts. Analyzing present day experiences through the eyes of science can also indicate that reports from the past, including the biblical appearances of Jesus Christ to his first disciples, can be regarded as real.

Because of the importance that visual encounters with Jesus had throughout history, professor Phillip Wiebe of Trinity Western University in Canada performed a study to investigate the appearances of Jesus Christ in the present day. The study was later published by Oxford Academic Press under the title *Visions of Jesus*. Wiebe conducted his research between 1988 and 1993, and analyzed thirty accounts from the United States, Canada, Australia and the U.K. In these experiences, (1) people were wide awake at the time of their encounter, (2) their eyes were open, and (3) they knew with absolute certainty that it was Jesus Christ who appeared before them. Wiebe excluded from his study near-death experiences and focused exclusively on studying those accounts where Jesus appeared visually to people under normal circumstances and in unexpected moments of their daily lives. "This list of exclusions alone gives an indication of how rich and varied such experiences are," writes Wiebe. Modern day encounters with Jesus Christ have transformed people's lives instantly and some of them even left physical evidence behind.

Patti Perior was only 9 years old when she was sent home from the hospital to die. She was suffering from three terminal illnesses, including a hole in her heart, and doctors couldn't do anything else to save her. Patti was put in isolation in her room, and nobody except her mother was allowed to enter. Late one night, Jesus Christ appeared at the foot of her bed saying, "I want you to tell your mother in the morning that you're going to be alright." "He was radiant," Patti recalls. "Light was emanating from his face and from his body. He was glorious. Love and truth were emanating from his eyes." The following day she was completely healed. Some years later in a conversation with her brother, she told him story of the night when Jesus appeared and healed her. To her surprise, her brother answered: "I know. I was peaking through the door of your bedroom and saw Jesus at the foot of your bed. I thought he'd come to take you to heaven."

Amy Ghazal grew up in a Muslim family in Syria. Her parents and the religious teachers in their community oftentimes beat Amy and told her that women are worthless. Amy moved to the United States where she married a Muslim doctor, but he begun abusing her and three years later they divorced. "I lost myself totally and felt like I have failed in everything," she recalls. "Why should I continue to live? I could not sleep and nobody wanted to be my friend because my face looked so depressed and miserable." She remembers holding "resentment all the time, against anybody." Several months later, Amy fell ill and was rushed to the emergency room. She was scheduled for surgery the following day. In the hospital room at night, she cried: "Jesus, I know you have healed a lot of people in the past. Would you please come and heal me if you are true? I am broken financially. I am alone. I don't have any family to care for me and I cannot survive by myself." "After I finished praying," she recalls, "the room was filled with light and out of that light Jesus [Christ] came to me in a real human body. He stretched his hands and he was close to me, saying "Come to me who are weary and carry heavy burdens and I will give you rest." Amy had never read the Bible nor had any idea these words are written in *The Gospel of Matthew.* "I saw nails in his wrists. Nobody will deny that he is God," she says. I felt dirty and full of sin. Jesus is holy, righteous and beautiful." The following morning doctors ran a series of tests before Amy's planned surgery, but found nothing wrong with her. She had been completely healed.

In 1973, Paul Trousdale, a successful real estate developer from California, was rushed to the hospital where doctors discovered he was bleeding internally and had lost a lot of blood. Medical treatments didn't improve his condition and some days later he lost blood pressure, broke out in a profuse sweat and lost consciousness. When he woke up the following day, his wife had come with a pastor from the local church. The pastor was standing at the right side of his bed and asked if they can pray together. Paul agreed and of a sudden Jesus Christ appeared standing by his left side. "I clearly saw Christ standing there and I was startled by it" he recalls. "He appeared in white robes, like the traditional paintings. I reached out my left hand. Christ took my hand and I felt the cold chill [in my body] leave. I felt that the bleeding stopped at that moment." Paul grabbed Jesus's hand and "a warm feeling flowed through my body," he remembers. "I was completely healed." The doctors did not believe him and refused to let him go home, but when they took a whole suite of tests, they found nothing. Paul was completely healed. His case is documented in Dr. Richard Casdorph's book *The Miracles*.

Dr. Nasir Siddiki, a Muslim from a high-class family, was admitted into a hospital in Toronto, Canada with a severe disease. His immune system had shut down and doctors said he was going to die by the following morning. In utter despair, Nasir cried out "God if you're real, don't let me die!" In the late hours of the night, a being of light appeared into his room. "I knew he was Jesus" Siddiki recalls. "I am the God of the Christians, he said to me." Nasir was released from the hospital and soon was completely healed. He became an evangelist for Jesus Christ.

Sometimes the appearances of Jesus are shared. In 1958, John and Nathan were roommates at a Bible college in Texas. Nathan was sick with a virus. One night, his roommate John was praying for him and he opened his eyes to look at his friend lying in bed about eight feet away. John was startled to see someone standing over Nathan's bed, but he immediately identified the presence to be Jesus Christ. John was about to open his mouth to tell Nathan what he was seeing, when Jesus placed his hand on Nathan's forehead and disappeared. Nathan instantly jumped out of bed and shouted, "I've been healed!" He confessed he didn't see anyone in the room, but he felt somebody touching his forehead. John recalls the appearances of Jesus was definitely real.

Sherzad Suleiman was a telecommunication engineer in the Iraqi army. One day while he was working, Sherzad was kidnapped by terrorists who demanded money for his life. "Every two hours for three days they beat me with the AK-47s," he recalls. "They broke my nose and knee." On the third day, someone appeared in their midst. "I saw him and heard him, but the people didn't see him. He said, "I am Jesus. Go home." Sherzad remembers the terrorists talking and moving around him. "These people kidnapped me, are you serious? I said." Then all of a sudden the kidnappers started fighting with each other and one of them shot the other. "I just opened the door and walked outside, took a taxi and went home," recalls Sherzad. "When I arrived home after three days, my wife opened the door. "What happened to you?" she cried. "I saw Jesus in my dream. He told me, "I saved your husband. He is safe and coming home soon."

Sir Alister Hardy, Fellow of the Royal Society of London and founder of The Religious Experience Research Centre at the University of Wales, remarks: "These examples of apparitions seen by responsible citizens of the present day show us that we can accept the stories of the appearances of Jesus to those who had been close to him, felt his love while he was alive, without any damage to our intellectual integrity." Wiebe also concludes that "enough reports of Christ apparitions come from people with strong educational backgrounds to warrant serious attention to the whole body of evidence." Skeptics must bare the question why would top professionals risk their reputation and career to publicly testify about encountering Jesus Christ unless something dramatic had happened in their lives? Some of the most respected scientists of the twenty-first century testify about their visual encounter with Jesus Christ.

Dr. James Tour is a professor of Materials Science and NanoEngineering and professor of Computer Science at Rice University in Texas. Tour is recognized among "The 50 Most Influential Scientists in the World Today" and was named "Scientist of the Year" in 2013. He works in the scientific group of a Nobel prize winner in chemistry and has lectured at every major university in America. With 650 research publications and 120 patents for inventions, Tour was ranked among the top 10 chemists in the world in the last decade and was inducted in the National Academy of Inventors in 2015. He received several prestigious awards for his scientific discoveries, including the Feynman Prize in Nanotechnology and the NASA Space Act Award in 2008. "On November 7, 1977 I was all alone in my room," he recalls. "I said, Lord Jesus, I am a sinner, please come into my life. Forgive me. All of a sudden, someone was in my room. I was on my knees and I opened my eyes. Jesus Christ stood in my room. I wasn't scared, I was just weeping. The presence was so glorious. I didn't want to get up. This amazing sense of forgiveness started to come upon me. I didn't know what to do. What means the most to me" Tour confessed, "is that I am a Jew who believes that Jesus Christ is the Savior" of the world.

Dr. Rich Flashman is a Jewish professor from New York City. "On April 30, 1980 I was in the parking lot of the Temple Sinai in Massachusetts with a cigarette and a coffee just thinking about life" he recalls. "I started thinking about Jewish history. Is Jesus the Christ? Is Jesus the Son of God? Is he God? What difference does it make what the name of God is as long as we live a good life? I'm thinking these things and walking around the parking lot. I get to the end of the parking lot and I look up, and before me is a gathering of light. The light forms into the figure of a man, and the man is all in light. He was in front of a cross. Not on the cross, but in front of the cross, brightly illuminated in front of me. I looked up, saw the figure and said 'Oh my God, it is Jesus Christ.' It scared me so much that I decided to put it out of my mind. I spent the next couple of weeks partying and going out to bars, trying to forget what had happened. I woke up one morning and my mother looked at me saying, "Rich, what are you running from?" I now realize there is a God, He loves me and His love sets me free to love and serve others."

The cumulative testimonies of Jesus Christ appearing all over the world demonstrate that these experiences are happening more often than we know. People from all walks of life - thieves and drug dealers, children and single moms, professors and academics, renowned scientists and terrorists, believers and unbelievers, ministers and atheists alike testify about Jesus Christ visibly appearing to them. Wiebe noted that these experiences are never generated by deliberate efforts to produce them through meditation, fasting, prayer or other techniques. Quite the contrary, data show that Jesus appears to people only when he wants, not whey they want, according to his will.

Margaret confessed she was an atheist. In 1952 she was having a conversation with her husband and a friend in their house in Australia when she felt compelled to turn and look towards the kitchen door. A few feet away was a figure she immediately recognized as Jesus Christ. Streams of liquid love poured from his eyes. The stillness of the moment seemed to her as a fragment of eternity. Margaret testified that this experience remained in her memory forty years later just as if it happened today.

One day when she was in church in Canada, Sheila saw Jesus Christ walking out of minister's office. He walked to the center of the podium and told her, "live by my commandments." She turned toward her friends to see if they were seeing what she was seeing, but they didn't show any signs that they were. She wondered if she was hallucinating and looked again to where Jesus was standing. He told her, "I'm here." She declared that she had no doubt about who she was seeing. The sense of love and beauty emanating from Jesus was overwhelming. Sheila confessed that Jesus Christ became very real to her after this encounter.

In 1991, Denny was with his my brother-in-law at their cabin in the mountains. "I went to bed around 10 o'clock, on a night like any other," he recalls. "I was in bed and a white light begun to accumulate in the corner of my bedroom where the walls meet the ceiling. The light grew. It exploded into intensity and fully engulfed the room. It wasn't just light, but there was music and a presence of love in the light. I remember thinking that we have a fireplace in the cabin, and before you go to bed you have to open a window or smoke can build up inside. If that happens, you can die. I thought to myself that I forgot to open the window and I died or I was dying. I was trying to rationalize what was happening when I saw a figure descending from the light. Every hair on my body stood up. I was electrified. I wasn't religious, I didn't know Jesus, but I knew in an instant that he was there. It was humbling. I turned away because I felt unworthy to look at him. I felt dirty. The way I led my life came before my eyes and it wasn't pleasant. I looked away and remember asking him to forgive me. I told him I loved him. He forgave me for all the stupid things I have done in my life. Why Jesus came to me, I don't know. I've done nothing but hurt what he tried to do for me. He was light and part of the light."

One of the most extraordinary features of the encounters with Jesus Christ is the absolute certainty people exhibit regarding the identity of the one standing before them. Most recognize Jesus instantly. His historical appearance is unknown and the physical descriptions reported over centuries vary, but nonetheless, people instantly know it is Jesus Christ who appears to them.

Helen was in her early twenties. One day when she was in church praying with her eyes closed, she felt somebody touching the hand she held raised in prayer. She opened her eyes, but nobody was around. She then looked up and saw Jesus Christ standing there, just as clear as she could see the other people in the church. He stretched his hands towards her and smiled. Jesus seemed so real, with a radiant glow surrounding him, that Helen wondered why other people were not looking at him too. The experience created in Helen the desire to please Jesus as much as she could. She recalls, "Jesus is not just something you learn about in a Bible or isn't just a story. [Jesus] showed me that he was real, that he is a real person. He's not just an apparition or a figment of our imagination. Nobody has been able to tell me since that Jesus isn't real."

Eve was the single mother of two teenage daughters. Unemployed and desperate about her situation, Eve felt that God was not aware of her need and she even questioned His existence. In a moment of despair, she knelt by her bed and raised her hands. "If I could only touch you. If I could only touch your hand," she cried out. She opened her eyes and was startled to see Jesus Christ in front of her. She recalls, "Jesus was on his knees holding both of my hands with the most compassionate, warm eyes I had ever seen, but with strength behind them. He was where the bed would have been." Before she felt comforted she got scared and ran out of the room.

4.

The phenomena occurring today can be seen as part of a continuous history of similar accounts that began with the post-resurrection appearances of Jesus Christ recorded in the gospels.

John had a vision of Jesus Christ on the island of Patmos in Greece. He wrote around the year 95 AD in *The Book of Revelation*: "When I saw [Jesus], I fell at His feet like a dead man. But He placed His right hand on me and said, "Do not be afraid. I am the First and the Last, the Living One. I was dead and behold, now I am alive forever and ever!"

Dr. T.L. Osborn, author and evangelist with a ministry spanning over sixty years, recalls the day when Jesus Christ appeared to him in 1947. "In the morning, at 6 o'clock sharp, Jesus walked into my bedroom. Not on the floor, but in the air. His eyes were like blazes of blue fire burning with love. I looked at him just as I looked at my wife, as I look at anybody. He was real. He stood there before me. I lay at his feet as a dead man. I couldn't move a finger or a toe. Water poured out of my eyes, yet I wasn't conscious of crying. The physical body could not stand his presence. I laid there until 2 o'clock in the afternoon. When I got up, I knew one thing. I knew Jesus Christ is alive."

In 1987, Charles Ndifon was in a church in Nigeria where the pastor was giving students the blessing to serve in the ministry. "When the young man laid his hands on me," Charles recalls, "everything disappeared and Jesus was standing in front of me as clearly as you are sitting in front of me. It wasn't a vision inside my head or something I had imagined. I didn't close my eyes, but I stared straight into the face of Jesus Christ. I couldn't endure his presence, it was so powerful that I cried. He isn't just a historical person in a book, I knew Jesus was alive. He walked straight into me and I fell over like a dead man. My body felt as if it had red hot coals inside and I was about to explode. When I got up three hours later my shirt was drenched in tears. Jesus looked like a Jewish man. It was like seeing Love walking. His eyes could see right through you. You couldn't hide anything from him. He could see everything."

James Maloney was only a teenager when he came to the point where he didn't want to live anymore. He became suicidal at fourteen years old. On December 31, 1970, he cried out to God: "If you're real, if you love me, reveal yourself to me. I need to know that I am accepted for who I am!" The next day, on January 1, 1971, a brilliant light appeared in his bedroom. "The light was beyond human description," James recalls, "and somebody was standing in that light. Two hands came out towards me from the light and when I looked I knew they were the hands of Jesus Christ. He spoke audibly to me and said, "I've heard your cry for acceptance and I've heard your cry for reality. I love you the way you are."

5.

Eyewitness testimonies are oftentimes neglected by skeptics despite their importance in how knowledge is acquired. Dr. C.A.J. Coady, professor of Philosophy at the University of Melbourne, Australia noted that the English law tradition requires formal testimonies to be first-hand and the persons who offer the testimonies to have the relevant authority, competence and credentials to do so. In the case for Jesus's appearances, "the important conditions for formal testimony are readily met by most of the first-hand reports," writes Wiebe. Charles Babbage, the father of the modern computer and professor of mathematics at Cambridge University wrote regarding eyewitness testimonies in the endeavors of science: "Where a significant number of witnesses grow without prior collusion, an event's probability increases sufficiently to overturn any biases against it." The continuously growing confluence of multiple, independent and reliable witnesses increases the probability of the testimony's accuracy.

"There are several features of [the modern day appearances of Jesus Christ] I find particularly thought-provoking," Wiebe continues. "The first is their extraordinary variety. A careful scrutiny of the accounts that have come down to us in history would probably have revealed this variety, but only upon being confronted with the contemporary experiences did I come to appreciate their variety and complexity." Moreover, the data about these apparitions are semi-experimental, meaning that although the phenomena didn't take place in a laboratory environment, it occurs repeatedly, in many circumstances, in many places, to many people from all over the world, over a long period of time. These occurrences cannot be repeated in lab settings, but semi-experimental data is equally valid and points to the truth. The "evidence for Christ's visions and apparitions is substantial given the reports of the last two thousand years," writes Wiebe, including the appearances documented in the present day.

On September 25, 2012, police officer Ali Perez lead his team into an apartment building where a suspect was assumed to be hiding. "I kicked the door," remembers Perez and the guy immediately fired a shotgun. The first bullet ripped a hole through Perez's left arm. He collapsed between the police officers and the suspect shooting at each other. His colleagues pulled back and Perez was left alone with the gunman. "I was having a very hard time coming to terms with the fact that this is where I was going to die," Ali recalls. "I expected a bullet to my head at any moment." Perez was lying on the ground when the suspect came toward him, but then "our Lord and Savior Jesus Christ was there, standing between us. Lord, I trust you completely, I said, what do you want me to do? Jesus picked up a feather and wrote something down. I watched this note fly off like a leaf. I followed it with my eyes and it landed on my chest. "I want you to bless him," said the note. This guy just shot a hole through my body, shot my supervisor, horribly molested two girls, and Jesus told me to bless him. I look at him and said "God bless you brother." The gunman instantly changed his behavior and asked Perez if he wanted to leave the apartment. He nodded yes and the suspect helped him to the door before he surrendered.

Ernie was born in 1930 in the slums of Halifax, Canada and grew up in a violent environment of alcoholism, physical hurt and emotional abuse. His mother taught him how to steal when he was only eight years old. After an armed robbery, young Ernie was locked in a detention center for boys where he was beaten and sexually molested several times. He then spent a combined sentence of 25 years in different maximum security prisons across the United States and Canada for theft, robbery, five escapes from jail and an attempt to murder a police officer. While Ernie was in prison, a certain Mr. Bailey came to visit him and told him that only God could change his life. Ernie responded with contempt, but Mr. Bailey drove six hours every month for the next eighteen months to urge Ernie to read the Bible and surrender his life to Jesus Christ. On March 12, 1975, Ernie woke up at 2 o'clock in the morning with the sense that he should ask God to forgive him. He knelt down in his cell to pray and when he stood up, Jesus Christ appeared in the doorway and walked towards him. Jesus placed his hand on his left shoulder, which Ernie physically felt, and told him three things. "First Jesus said," recalls Ernie, "I'm glad you didn't kill that police officer." Then he said, "your slate is now wiped clean." Last, "you can start all over again." Jesus then disappeared. Twenty five years in prison and forty five years of sin wiped clean in a face to face encounter with Jesus Christ. One year later, on April 14, 1976 Ernie walked out the penitentiary as a free man. To this day, the government of Canada cannot tell who is responsible for Ernie having been released from prison.

The appearances of Jesus Christ are definitely not vivid mental pictures produced at will by imagining or concentrating on sensory information previously experienced such as religious paintings, or perhaps by closing one's eyes, breathing techniques or ingesting mind-altering substances. People who encounter Jesus Christ have little control over the onset, duration or content of their experience. Dr. James Gibson, American psychologist and one of the most renowned scientists in the field of visual perception, discovered that our five senses work together in order for us to relate to and understand our environment. The systems involved in perception - (1) the orienting system that allows us to determine the position of our bodies, (2) the visual system, (3) the auditory system, (4) the system of taste and smell, and (5) the haptic system of touch - are interrelated and work together. In the case of Christ's appearances, these systems are active and function normally. People are aware of their position whether standing, kneeling, falling down, they visually see Jesus, hear his voice, feel his touch and some even smell a wonderful fragrance. During their encounter, their perception system is operating as usual. In some accounts people even have conversations with Jesus Christ.

Javid Afshin is an Islamic terrorist who participated in executions of Christians. He was arrested for carrying illegal passports and imprisoned in Malaysia. One night in the cell, "I felt the whole room filled with the holy presence of God," he recalls. "It was as if time stopped. You know things about God without Him saying anything to you. The first thing I knew about God was His holiness. I knew He is just and I immediately knew that I am alone. In spite of all the good things I have done, I knew I had sins in my life. Then I felt a touch on my left shoulder and a voice said "I forgive you." I didn't understand how could this be possible. I asked "Who are you that forgives me so that I feel forgiven?" He answered, "I am the way, the truth and the life." I did not understand what this means because I had never heard these words before. "What is your name?" I asked, to which he answered "Jesus Christ, the Living God." I fell on the floor and just wept. Eighteen years later, I still can't forgive his love and his mercy."

Ron was raised in an abusive environment in California. At thirteen he was taking drugs and by the time he graduated from high school he had become a drug dealer. "I became violent," Ron recalls. "I carried weapons and guns everywhere I went." Years passed and although "I drove fancy cars and had the cash in my pocket," he was "very empty on the inside. I just couldn't seem to get out of it. One night I was sitting in my house and said, "God, if You're really real, help me. I can't get out of this life. I hate it. I don't want to live anymore." The following evening Ron was arrested and put in prison. In the night in the county jail, "Jesus Christ appeared to me as real as you are," Ron recalls. "I said, what do you want? He said, "You," to which I answered, "You can't want someone like me. I've done all these things, hurt all these people." Jesus said, "I came for people like you," then he disappeared. Ron called his family, and his mother and grandmother bailed him out of jail and took him straight to church."I dropped on my knees and started crying 'cause I was such a mess. I prayed to receive Jesus Christ into my heart as my Savior, and I was delivered from drugs immediately."

Marian was devastated by her son's death in a car accident. After the funeral, Marian locked herself in his room to be surrounded by the memories of her lost child. She laid in his bed and became angry with God, demanding to know why He took her son away. The following morning she was with her family members in the living room praying, when the back door flew open and a breeze swept through the house. Suddenly a light brighter that the Sun filled the room. Jesus Christ stepped out of the light and came into view. He stretched his hand towards her and told her took look at his arm. Marian noticed four children running on a green hill, one of them being the son she had just lost. Jesus spoke to Marion, "Look past [your son], Joe. Have you forgotten them? They are with me." Then Marian realized the other three children were the three pregnancies she had lost many years before.

Another case investigated by Wiebe is that of John who grew up Connecticut. At some point during high school, John turned away from God. Since then, for the next twenty six years, he was filled with hatred towards Jesus Christ. He walked into churches and cursed the Christ on the crucifix, or bawled at him to come down from the cross so that he could beat him up. Later on in life, John joined the U.S. Air Force as an engineer, but became an alcoholic and by the age of forty his body was nearly destroyed. In 1984, a friend advised John to pray and repent for his sins. He agreed to do so. Suddenly, an overwhelming feeling of heaviness came upon him. John cried out to God and asked for forgiveness for everything he had done in the past. The room was flooded with light. He recalls the wall was shinning brighter than the Sun, but he could still look at it without burning his eyes. Jesus Christ appeared in the midst of the light. John recalls a sense of love and compassion coming upon him as Jesus stretched his hands towards him.

The contemporary encounters with Jesus Christ corroborate and validate the testimonies of the Bible. *The Gospel of Matthew* describes the following account, similar to the pattern of the modern day ones: "Jesus took with him Peter, James and John the brother of James, and led them up a high mountain by themselves. There he was transfigured before them. His face shone like the sun and his clothes became as white as the light."

Scholars agree that the appearances of Jesus Christ are real encounters. "There are many accounts of extraordinary events for which no adequate materialistic explanations exist," says Dr. Wiebe. "The problem is remarkable inasmuch as nobody doubts the visions of Christ. This point is acknowledged by everyone, even by the most adamant opponents of supernaturalism." Other kinds of paranormal phenomena are readily rejected by science, but the apparitions of Jesus Christ are universally accepted in the academic world. Similar to how near-death experiences have grown to be widely accepted in the scholarly environment, the appearances of Jesus Christ are becoming more accepted by science because the evidence available is generous for research. Studying the apparitions of Jesus Christ, however, cannot be done according to the classical standards of scientific inquiry, the demand for repeated measurements, the control of parameters and variables, laboratory experiments and quantitative analysis to test the theories. His "apparitions threaten both the hegemony of physicalism and the supremacy of the scientific standards of inquiry, but this doesn't make them not true" writes Wiebe. Collecting reports and testimonies from living subjects, as opposed to ancient documents, holds extraordinary value for science. William James, the father of modern psychology, commented that the apparitions of Jesus Christ provide additional evidence for the resurrection beyond that provided by the New Testament accounts.

Some people question why Jesus appears to some and not to others. The Bible answers: "God allowed [Jesus] to appear, not to the general public, but to us whom God has chosen in advance to be his witnesses." Jesus Christ appears to people by the will of God, not by the choice of men.

The Gospel of John documents the following encounter several days after Jesus was crucified. "Thomas called Didymus was not with the disciples when Jesus came. So the other disciples told him, "We have seen the Lord!" But he replied, "Unless I see the nail marks in his hands, and put my finger where the nails have been and put my hand into his side, I will never believe." Eight days later, his disciples were once again inside with the doors locked and Thomas was with them. Jesus came and stood among them and said, "Peace be with you." Then Jesus said to Thomas, "Put your finger here and look at my hands. Reach out your hand and put it into my side. Stop doubting and believe." Thomas replied, "My Lord and my God!" Jesus said to him, "Because you have seen me, you have believed; blessed are those who have not seen and yet have believed." Considering the ever-growing data gathered through the centuries confirming that Jesus Christ still shows himself to people from all walks of life, the question is do you believe?

CHAPTER 7

The Breath of Life

Q7 - Who is Jesus called the Christ?

"I am the Beginning and the End.
The First and the Last."

For the open minds hungry for reality, modern science points with ever increasing evidence that the mystery of Jesus Christ is greater than anything else in this universe. Jesus is a historical figure who lived in the first century Judea, and his words and deeds are documented in the books of the Bible. Contemporary medical science confirms with remarkable evidence that Jesus Christ still heals the sick and raises the dead today. Irrespective of any prior beliefs regarding the supernatural, his name still has the power to cast out demons and set people free from physical, mental and emotional oppression, while the professional health community is growing more aware of the reality of the spiritual dimension. Data and academic research continues to reveal that Jesus Christ still appears alive to people from all walks of life regardless of their religion, traditions or spiritual beliefs. Two thousand years after his death and resurrection, Jesus still restores the brokenhearted and gives new life and new beginnings to those who call upon him with a truthful heart. The increasing number of corroborating testimonies confirm that heaven is a real place and Jesus Christ is alive in the afterlife. He meets those who passed on and saves from hell those whom he decides to give a second chance to. The last question of this mystery is "who is Jesus called the Christ?" Some people believe he was a moral teacher, while others say he was a prophet or a healer. Some regard Jesus as a religious leader, while others believe Christ is some kind of consciousness we can attain through various spiritual practices. None of these beliefs, however, even closely match the contemporary data nor what Jesus Christ declared about himself. What did his own words reveal about him? What did those who spent three years with

Jesus learned about him? And probably the most important question of all is, "why does Jesus Christ matter for every person alive today?"

1. Jesus Christ knows everything about everyone throughout the eternity of time.

- Nobody can hide anything from Jesus. He is the one "who searches minds and hearts." He has access to everyone's innermost thoughts, and "there is nothing hidden that will not be revealed and nothing secret that will not be made known."

- Jesus knows personally and intimately every person who has ever lived. He knows each and every one by name. Those who belong to God "hear my voice and I know them," says Jesus.

- Jesus knows every secret in the heart of man and knows every action every person has ever done on the face of this earth. "Jesus would not entrust himself to them for he knew all people," writes apostle John. "He knew what was in each person." On the day when we will stand before him, all our secret thoughts and deeds will come out into the open.

- Jesus has complete authority from God to give us eternal life, to bring us into heaven or cast us into hell. He urges all people throughout history to be exclusively concerned with how God regards them rather than with how other people see them. "Do not be afraid of them who kill the body. They are not able to kill the soul. But fear Him who is able to destroy both soul and body in hell." To fulfill his words, Jesus must have the same power and authority as God.

- Jesus Christ will judge every person that has ever lived. God "judges no one, but has passed all judgement to the Son." Every individual who has ever lived will face Jesus in judgement.

- Jesus Christ has the authority to present us before the living God or to take us away from His presence. "Whoever makes me known in front of men, I will make him known to my Father in heaven." To fulfill his words, Jesus must be in heaven, alive forever, know every single moment in the life of each person, and hold the same authority as God over people.

2. Jesus Christ is present with every person throughout history.

- "Wherever two or three [believers] gather in my name, there am I with them," Jesus promised. He can fulfill his words only if he lives forever, knows everything about everyone, and is present in all places at all times, something which only God can do.

- Jesus is present with every person who believes in him throughout history. "I am with you each and every day until the end of the age," he promised. Jesus can fulfill these words only if he is present everywhere at all times and intimately knows every one of us. He didn't say he will be in our memory or in our thoughts, but that he will be personally present in our daily lives.

- Jesus Christ has the power to protect all those who follow him, "those who have been called, who are loved by God the Father and kept safe by Jesus Christ," writes Jude. Jesus can fulfill this promise only if he is present everywhere, he is alive in every moment in history and has the power and authority to change the life circumstances of every person who obeys him.

- "I will not leave you as orphans. I will come to you," promised Jesus. To be able to fulfill his words, Jesus must be present everywhere at all times, to know the hidden desires of every person on the face of the earth and to be able to be present with all those who call on his name.

3. Jesus Christ has complete power and authority over every person who has ever lived.

- Jesus promises to comfort, heal and restore every person who chooses to believe in him. "Come to me all and I will give you rest," he says. "You will find rest for your souls." Jesus promises to heal the mind, emotions and heart of every person throughout history who decides to believe in him. To fulfill his words, Jesus must have access to the inner world of each individual, to know everything about everyone, and have power over each person alive.

- Jesus Christ has the willingness, ability and resources to fulfill every request of those who trust in him, who have him as their life source and ask aligned with the will of God. "If you get your life from me and my words live in you, ask whatever you want. It will be done for you." In order to fulfill his promise, Jesus Christ must hold the power to orchestrate the life circumstances of every person who believes in him, to personally and intimately know each and every one of us, and be present everywhere in every moment throughout history.

- Jesus has complete power and authority over the eternal destiny of each person on this planet. God "granted him authority over all people that he might give them eternal life." Jesus gives a serious warning that every single individual will one day stand before him in judgement. Regardless of their country, religion, cultural traditions or spiritual beliefs, every human being will go through a life review with Jesus. Every intent of the heart and every work will be exposed, and all will be rewarded or punished according to their works.

- Jesus Christ has the ability, authority and choice to resurrect people from the dead and give them eternal life. As God "raises the dead," Jesus also "gives life to anyone he chooses."

- Jesus has the authority to decide who will spend eternity with him in heaven, and he also has the power to throw people into hell. Jesus doesn't care about what people do using his name. He is interested in us doing God's will which is to believe in Jesus Christ, and have a personal relationship with him. "Not everyone who says to me, 'Lord, Lord,' will enter the kingdom of heaven, but he who does the will of My Father who is in heaven will enter. Many will say to me on that day, 'Lord, Lord, did we not prophesy in your name, and in your name cast out demons, and in your name perform many miracles?' And then I will declare to them, "I never knew you, depart from me, you who practice lawlessness." Jesus wants you to know him.

- Jesus Christ made it possible for every person in history to receive a new life that will last forever, something only God can do. "Whoever puts his trust in Him will have eternal life."

- Jesus Christ is the very source of life. He promises to nourish the mind and heart of every single person who comes to him throughout history. "I am the Bread of Life," declares Jesus. He who comes to me will never be hungry. He who believes in me will never be thirsty."

- God has made people the personal property of Jesus Christ. "All whom my Father has given me will come to me."

- Jesus promised to receive every person who chooses to believe in him regardless of what they have done in the past. "I will never turn away anyone who comes to me."

- Jesus Christ came from heaven to fulfill God's will to save people from this evil world. "The Father sent me. He did not want me to lose any of all those he gave me." God wants everyone to put their trust in Jesus and receive the gift of eternal life that only Christ will give us."

- Jesus is not one of the many religious leaders of humanity. Others might teach good morals, but "Jesus Christ is the one appointed by God to be the judge of all the living and the dead."

4. Jesus Christ has total power and authority over everything in the universe.

- God, the Creator of the universe, has given Jesus complete authority over nature. "Everything the Father has is mine," declares Jesus. "All things have been committed to me by my Father." The universe, our planet and everything in it is the personal property of Jesus Christ.

- Everything in this universe, galaxies, planets, the earth with all its life forms and every human being who's ever lived was created by Jesus Christ, with no exceptions whatsoever. "Through him all things were made and apart from him nothing was made that has been made."

- God offered to Jesus Christ "the nations [as his] inheritance, the ends of the earth [as his possession]." Jesus rules over all presidents, kings and queens, and all human authorities set over the nations of this earth. He is the "King of Kings and Lord of Lords."

- Jesus himself is the total wisdom of God. In Christ "are hidden all the treasures of wisdom and knowledge." Those who seek for wisdom with a truthful heart will always find Jesus Christ.

- God has given Jesus Christ complete power and authority to rule over everyone and everything in the universe. "All power is given unto him in heaven and on earth." Jesus owns the universe and everything contained in it. "There was given him dominion, and all nations should serve him. He will have rulership and dominion and glory forever. All people will worship him."

- Jesus Christ has the power to change everything in the universe. "I am making everything new," he promises, "a new heaven and a new earth." "This world is passing away" and every person alive should be primarily concerned with saving their souls rather than the planet.

- Just as a builder is greater than the house he builds, Jesus Christ is above his creation. He requires all people to listen to him and obey his words because "heaven and earth will pass away, but my words will never pass away." Jesus must come before everything else in life.

5. Angels are the personal property of Jesus Christ.

- Jesus "has gone into heaven and is at the right hand of God with angels, authorities and powers in submission to him." All angels and spirits are under the authority and rulership of Jesus.

- Jesus will personally send his angels to earth to punish every single person in history who rejected him, acted wickedly and lived against the will of God. Jesus "will send out his angels and they will weed out of his kingdom everything that causes sin and all who do evil. They will throw them into the blazing furnace where there will be weeping and gnashing of teeth."

- In heaven, "ten thousand times ten thousand, and thousands of thousands" of angels are around the throne of Jesus Christ and worship him, saying "worthy is the Lamb who was slain to receive power and riches and wisdom, and strength and honor and glory and blessing!"

- Jesus Christ sends his angels to whomever he wishes to bring revelation and commandments from heaven. "I, Jesus, have sent my angel" to bring you wisdom and the knowledge of God.

6. Jesus Christ requires absolute loyalty from every person who has ever lived.

- Jesus requires every person to make him their main priority in life, above everything and everyone else. "Anyone who loves their father or mother more than me is not worthy of me, and anyone who loves their son or daughter more than me is not worthy of me," he tells us.

- Jesus Christ is the only one who has opened up the possibility for each person who has ever lived to become a member of God's family. "To all who did receive him," writes apostle John, "to those who believed in his name, [Jesus] gave the right to become children of God."

- Jesus informs people that if they are ashamed of him before others, he will personally take away their inheritance in the afterlife. He gives a serious warning to all people that "whoever acknowledges me before others, I will also acknowledge before my Father in heaven. But whoever disowns me before others, I will disown before my Father in heaven."

- Because God and Jesus are one and the same, Jesus Christ requires people to honor him as they honor God, the creator the universe. He tells people that those who dishonor him dishonor God, and those who hate him hate God himself.

- Jesus teaches people to receive him as their only source of life. It is his very presence in us that gives us eternal life. "Get your life from me. Then I will live in you and you will give much fruit. You can do nothing without me."

- Jesus informs people that those who sincerely search for the truth will always find him. He plainly declares that all spiritual paths and world's religions are lies that "lead to destruction," but those who genuinely seek the truth will always find him. Throughout history, "everyone who is of the truth hears my voice," says Jesus.

7. Jesus Christ was sent by God to give people eternal life.

- Jesus informs people that he was sent by God to pay for the sins and evil done by every person who has ever lived, and thus give everyone the chance to enter heaven and receive eternal life. He says that "God so loved the world that He gave [Jesus], His only begotten son, that whoever believes in him should not perish but have everlasting life. For God did not send His son into the world to condemn the world, but that the world through him might be saved."

- Jesus Christ came to earth from eternity because he loves each person individually and wants all of us to be with him forever in heaven. He says, "I left the Father and came into the world. Now I am leaving the world and going back to the Father. I will come back and take you to be with me that you also may be where I am." Jesus sacrificed his life because "I want those you have given me to be with me where I am."

- Jesus Christ has the ability and authority to resurrect people from the dead and to give eternal life to every individual throughout history who calls on his name. In doing this, Jesus fulfills God's plan because "my Father's will is that everyone who looks to the Son and believes in him shall have eternal life and I will raise them up at the last day."

- People who choose to trust in Jesus Christ as their Lord and Savior "will never be punished for their sins." Those who believe in Jesus "hear my voice and they follow me. I give them eternal life" and they become God's own.

- Jesus Christ has absolute power and dominion over every demonic, earthly or heavenly being. Demons wage war to destroy people, but "no one is able to take them out of my hand," declares Jesus. "My Father who gave them to me is greater than all. No one is able to take them out of my Father's hand." Jesus Christ has the power to keep people safe forever.

- Jesus is "the one who raises the dead and gives them life." He plainly promised that "anyone [throughout history] who puts his trust in me will live again, even if he dies."

8. Jesus Christ is the very life force that resurrects the dead to eternal life.

- Jesus is the power that raises the dead from the grave. Regardless of when people die, Christ has the ability to resurrect them to eternal life because he is "the resurrection and the life."

- Jesus Christ is the very breath of life by which everything lives. "I am the life," he declares.

- Just as God has life eternal, so does Jesus Christ have everlasting life. "As the Father has life in himself, so He has granted the Son also to have life in himself." God has given Jesus the power, the authority and the choice to give eternal life to whomever he wants. "For as the Father raises the dead and gives them life, even so the Son gives life to whom he will."

9. Jesus Christ is the only way to God because Jesus is God.

- *The Gospel of John* documents the most extraordinary statement a person who lived on this earth has ever made: "No one comes to the Father except through me." In one sentence, Jesus declares that all religious systems are false, condemns the idea people have that many spiritual paths lead to God as completely wrong, and apprises us that only He can grant us access into heaven. People may point the way to God, but Jesus Christ doesn't point the way. He states it plainly that he is the exclusive way for people to come into the presence of the living God.

- Jesus reiterated the warning that he is the only way to God by saying that all people who truly hear God's voice will come to him, while all other teachings lead people astray to demons and destruction. If what people learn doesn't draw them to Jesus, then what they've heard didn't come from God. "Everyone who has heard the Father and learned from Him comes to me."

- Jesus Christ is the only Son of God who was born into the world for all people to see and know God personally. "Whoever has seen me," says Jesus, "has seen the Father." "No one has ever seen God but the one and only Son, who is himself God, who has made Him known."

- Apostle Paul gives a solemn warning that regardless of how people doubt or reject Jesus Christ, the day is coming when "at the name of Jesus every knee will bow." On that day, every single person in history, without exception, "will confess that Jesus Christ is Lord."

- Jesus has the ability, authority and personal choice to reveal the reality of God to whomever he wishes. He instructs people that nobody can reach or know God without Christ making it possible. Nobody finds God through mental powers, meditations, affirmations or other man-made techniques. "No man knows God except the one to whom the Son will reveal Him." People might mentally accept the existence of God, but nobody can know God without Jesus revealing Him to them.

- Jesus Christ is God on earth. He is the visible image of the living God. Those who want to know how God is like must look to Jesus Christ. Jesus "was in the beginning with God," before galaxies, planets and everything in the universe was created. "He existed before" time begun, before the first human being was born on the earth. Jesus has no past and no future. He is the great I AM, alive, the same yesterday, today and forever."

- The name of Jesus is the name of God. "Holy Father, you have given me *your* name." God Himself exalted Jesus Christ and had "given him a name above every other name."

- The name of Jesus Christ has the power and authority to protect those who believe in him throughout history. "I protected them by the power of the name You gave me."

- Jesus Christ is "the light of the world." He is the only one who has access to the mind and heart of each individual, and only Jesus can make people aware of the reality of God.

10. Jesus Christ will return to rule over the whole earth.

- Jesus Christ warned people in advance that his return to the earth will be an event of cosmic magnitude precedented by wars and natural disasters. Jesus foretold that before his coming, "nations will have wars with other nations. Countries will fight against countries. The earth will shake and break apart in different places. There will be no food. There will be bad diseases among many people. The nations of the earth will be troubled and will not know what to do. They will be troubled at the angry sea and waves." These events are already coming to pass and are unfolding faster with each passing year. Then, after "those days of trouble and pain and sorrow are over, the sun will get dark. The moon will not give light. The stars will fall from the sky." These signs foretell Jesus' second coming and "all nations will have sorrow."

- Jesus Christ will not return in secret to some mysterious place on earth, but on that day every person alive, whether they believed in him or not, and regardless of the country or city or village they live in will look up and see him "coming with his angels on the clouds of the sky."

- Jesus Christ will not return to earth as a human being, but as the Son of God, the creator and ruler of the universe. Every person, with no exception, will see Jesus with their own eyes coming "as lightning shines across the sky from east to west." Nobody knows the day, but every person on the face of the earth will see him "coming with power and great glory."

- Jesus Christ will personally send his angels to "gather God's people together" from every corner of the world and will place those who believed in him to "shine as the sun in the kingdom of their Father." He will destroy all who've done evil, who refused, mocked and rejected God. Unbelievers, those who sin and cause others to sin will be punished by his angels. Their suffering will be so terrible that there will be "loud crying and grinding of teeth."

- "The nations will be gathered before him," and every person who has ever lived will stand in judgement before Jesus. He will punish or reward people according to what they have done.

- Jesus Christ gives a solemn warning to all people who live on the face of the earth that "he who puts his trust in me and is baptized will be saved from the punishment of sin. But he who does not put his trust in me is guilty and will be punished forever."

11. Jesus Christ is the savior of the world.

- Jesus Christ loves all people with a "love that transcends human understanding." He came to the earth to sacrifice his life so that all who believe in him are "made free from sin." Jesus, as the Son of God, is the only one who could die for us and "take away the sin of the world."

- Jesus Christ made it possible for all people to be in communion with God and become his children. No human being can lead us back to God, except the only Son of God. The moment anyone believes in him, Jesus Christ gives that person eternal life. For God we are the most precious thing in the universe, because it cost God everything to redeem us from the power of sin and death.

- God forgives every sin only if we ask Him for forgiveness in the name of Jesus Christ. Jesus is the exclusive way for every person who lives on earth to be forgiven. "Men must repent for their sins and turn from them. Then they will be forgiven. This must be preached in His name, [the name of Jesus Christ] to all nations."

- Jesus Christ is the only one who has the authority, ability and power to give a new life and a new beginning to every person alive, regardless of their past and what they have done. Jesus is our only chance to begin life once more and live it right and make it beautiful. He has the power to wipe away all past, give us a new heart and a new future. "Anyone who belongs to Christ is a new being. The old life is gone. The new life has begun. This all is a gift from God."

- Jesus Christ came to earth to give birth to a new species of people that live united with God, a family that lives by the power of God's Holy Spirit. Jesus shared with us the glory God bestowed upon Him in order for us to become God's family united by faith and love. "I gave them the glory You gave me that they may be one as we are One," says Jesus.

- Jesus Christ gave to those who believe in him the supreme authority, responsibility and power to represent God on earth. Those who reject Christians reject Jesus Christ and God Himself. "Whoever listens to you, listens to me. Whoever has nothing to do with you, has nothing to do with me. Whoever has nothing to do with me, has nothing to do with the One Who sent me."

EPILOGUE

Jesus Christ is the breath of life. He is the Word through which God spoke the universe into existence, the only begotten Son of the living God who existed before everything was created. He is alive forevermore. Jesus Christ is the wisdom of God and the mystery of all knowledge is hidden in him. Jesus Christ is love. He loves every person on earth with an unfathomable love that he sacrificed his own life to pay for the sins of humanity and open the way to heaven for all who believe in him. Jesus Christ is the beginning and the end of all things, and everything in between. He is the meaning, the purpose and the life. Jesus hopes all things, believes all things, endures all things, and waits for every person to receive his sacrifice on the cross and God's gift of eternal life. Nobody can know Jesus Christ through the reasoning of the mind. To the world, Christ remains a mystery. Those who don't belong to him might investigate, analyze, categorize, rationalize, but they can never understand nor know Jesus through their mind. No human being can identify Jesus with his natural thinking, even though Christ is more real than everything else in this universe. Until you get on your knees, open your heart, ask him to forgive your sins and surrender your heart and your life to him, you will not know Jesus. Only Jesus can reveal himself in your heart, and until He reveals himself you will only know about him. But once you know him, you cannot un-know him. His very being will flood your heart with love, purpose and peace that transcends understanding. When you truly know Jesus Christ, your life will never be the same. His message for every person on this earth is simple: "Come to me, all…"

REFERENCES

Introduction

30 Days of Prayer for the Muslim World Project, https://www.30daysprayer.com, accessed January, 5, 2020

Anderlini, J., *The rise of Christianity in China,* Financial Times, 2014, https://www.ft.com/content/a6d2a690-6545-11e4-91b1-00144feabdc0, accessed January, 5, 2020

Brown, M., *7 Lessons From The World's Fastest Growing Congregation,* www.christianpost.com/news/7-lessons-from-the-worlds-fastest-growing-congregation-152310/, accessed January, 5, 2020

Calvary Temple in Hyderabad, Wikipedia, https://en.wikipedia.org/wiki/Calvary_Temple, accessed January, 5, 2020

Chapman, C., *Christians in the Middle East – Past, Present and Future,* Transformation: An International Journal of Holistic Mission Studies, https://doi.org/10.1177/0265378812439955, accessed January, 5, 2020

Christianity in its Global Context 1970–2020, Center for the Study of Global Christianity, Gordon-Conwell Theological Seminary, 2013, https://gordonconwell.edu/wp-content/uploads/sites/13/2019/04/2ChristianityinitsGlobalContext.pdf, accessed January, 5, 2020

Connor, P., *6 facts about South Korea's growing Christian population,* Pew Research, https://www.pewresearch.org/fact-tank/2014/08/12/6-facts-about-christianity-in-south-korea/, accessed January, 5, 2020

Crash: Yak Service YK42 at Yaroslavl on Sep 7th 2011 failed to climb on takeoff, The Aviation Herald, http://avherald.com/h?article=4428da13&opt=0, accessed January, 5, 2020

Garrison, D. *A Wind in the House Blog,* http://windinthehouse.org/category/blog/, accessed January, 5, 2020

Garrison, D., *A Wind in the House Of Islam: How God is Drawing Muslims Around the World to Faith in Jesus Christ,* WIGTake Resources, 2014

Global Christianity – A Report on the Size and Distribution of the World's Christian Population, Pew Research, 2011, https://www.pewforum.org/2011/12/19/global-christianity-exec/, accessed January, 5, 2020

Greeson, K., *The Camel: How Muslims Are Coming To Faith In Christ*, Wigtake Resources, 2010

Hernández, J.C., *As China Cracks Down on Churches, Christians Declare 'We Will Not Forfeit Our Faith,'* The New York Times, 2018, https://www.nytimes.com/2018/12/25/world/asia/china-christmas-church-crackdown.html, accessed January, 5, 2020

Johnson, T.M. et. al., *Christianity 2017: Five Hundred Years of Protestant Christianity*, International Bulletin of Mission Research 1–12, 2016, https://gordonconwell.edu/wp-content/uploads/sites/13/2019/04/IBMR2017.pdf, accessed January, 5, 2020

Kandiah, K., *The Church is Growing and Here are the Figures that Prove It*, 2015, https://www.christiantoday.com/article/a-growing-church-why-we-should-focus-on-the-bigger-picture/49362.htm, accessed January, 5, 2020

Lokomotiv Yaroslavl Plane Crash, including list of references, https://en.wikipedia.org/wiki/Lokomotiv_Yaroslavl_plane_crash, accessed January, 5, 2020.

MayDay / Air Crash Investigations, "Lokomotiv Hockey Team Disaster," aired March 4, 2013

Merriam Webster Dictionary, https://www.merriam-webster.com/dictionary/science, accessed January, 5, 2020

Paler, O., *Apărarea lui Galilei*, in Romanian, 1978

Phillips, T., *China on Course to Become World's Most Christian Nation within 15 years*, https://www.telegraph.co.uk/news/worldnews/asia/china/10776023/China-on-course-to-become-worlds-most-Christian-nation-within-15-years.html, accessed January, 5, 2020

Sanneh, L., *Disciples of All Nations: Pillars of World Christianity*, Oxford Studies in World Christianity, Oxford University Press, 2007

Sanneh, L., *Whose Religion Is Christianity? The Gospel Beyond the West*, Eerdmans, 2003

Seow, D., *Dr Satish Kumar: The Story Of A Church Built In 52 Days*, 2019, https://www.citynews.sg/2019/03/15/dr-satish-kumar-the-story-of-a-church-built-in-52-days/, accessed January, 5, 2020

Shackelford, J., *Burned alive: Giordano Bruno, Galileo and the Inquisition*, Annals of Science, DOI: 10.1080/00033790.2019.1604993, 2019

The Changing Global Religious Landscape Babies Born to Muslims will Begin to Outnumber Christian Births by 2035, Pew Research Center, 2017, http://assets.pewresearch.org/wp-content/

uploads/sites/11/2017/04/07092755/FULL-REPORT-WITH-APPENDIXES-A-AND-B-APRIL-3.pdf, accessed January, 5, 2020

The Explosion of Christianity in Africa, https://www.christianity.com/church/church-history/timeline/2001-now/the-explosion-of-christianity-in-africa-11630859.html, accessed January, 5, 2020

The Galileo Project, Rice University, http://galileo.rice.edu, accessed January, 5, 2020

The Global Religious Landscape, A Report on the Size and Distribution of the World's Major Religious Groups as of 2010, Pew Research, 2012, https://assets.pewresearch.org/wp-content/uploads/sites/11/2014/01/global-religion-full.pdf, accessed January, 5, 2020

The Holy Bible, multiple translations, https://www.biblegateway.com/

Todd M. et al., *Christianity 2018: More African Christians and Counting Martyrs,* International Bulletin of Mission Research, Vol. 42(1) 20–28, 2018

Yang, F., *Center on Religion and Chinese Society,* Purdue University, https://www.purdue.edu/crcs/, accessed January, 5, 2020

Yang, F., *On Christian Growth in China,* https://www.youtube.com/watch?v=jg78cbmBJoA, accessed January, 5, 2020

Chapter 1

Albright, W. F., *Recent Discoveries in Bible Lands,* Funk and Wagnalls, 1955

Bacchus F. J., *St. Polycarp,* Catholic Encyclopedia, Robert Appleton Company, 1911

Basore, J.W., *Dialogue "To Marcia on Consolation,"* in *Moral Essays,* 6.20.3, The Loeb Classical Library, Harvard University Press, 1946

Bauckham, R., *Jesus and the Eyewitnesses: The Gospels as Eyewitness Testimony,* Eerdmans, 2006

Benko, S., *Pagan Rome and the Early Christians,* Indiana University Press, 1986

Blomberg, C., *The Historical Reliability of the New Testament,* Crossway, 1994

Bruce, F. F., *The New Testament Documents: Are They Reliable?* InterVarsity, 1964

Bruce, F.F., *Archaeological Confirmation of the New Testament, Revelation and the Bible*, Carl Henry, Baker, 1969

Bucklin, R., *The Legal and Medical Aspects of the Trial and Death of Christ*, Med. Sci. Law. 10:14-26, 1970

Burridge, R., *What Are the Gospels? A Comparison with Graeco-Roman Biography,* Eerdmans, 2004

Carrington, P., *The Early Christian Church,* Volume 1, Cambridge University Press, 2011

Carson, D. A., Moo, D. J., Morris, L., *An Introduction to the New Testament,* Zondervan, 1992

Conway, C.M., *Behold the Man: Jesus and Greco-Roman Masculinity*, Oxford University, 2008.

Craig, W. L., *Reasonable Faith, Thallus on Darkness at Noon,* https://www.reasonablefaith.org/question-answer/P70/thallus-on-the-darkness-at-noon, 2010, accessed January, 6, 2020

Davis, C.T., *The Crucifixion of Jesus: The Passion of Christ from a Medical Point of View*, Ariz. Med. 22:183-187, 1965

Dunn, J. D. G., *Jesus Remembered: Christianity in the Making*, Eerdmans, 2003

Eastman, M., *The Agony of Love - Medical Aspects of the Crucifixion*, https://www.khouse.org/articles/1998/113/, 1998, accessed January, 5, 2020

Edwards, W. D. et al., *On the Physical Death of Jesus Christ,* JAMA, 255(11):1455-1463, 1986, https://jamanetwork.com/journals/jama/article-abstract/403315, accessed January, 6, 2020

Ehrman, B., *The New Testament: A Historical Introduction to the Early Christian Writings,* Oxford University Press, 2011. Ehrman accepts the scholarly conclusion that the gospels of the New Testament are examples of Greco-Roman biographies, but disagrees with their claims.

Eusebius, *Ecclesiastical History,* Book 3, chapter 39, 340 AD.

Eusebius, *Ecclesiastical History*, Book 4, Chapter 15, 340 AD

Evans, C., *Fabricating Jesus*, InterVarsity, 2006

France. R.T., *The Evidence for Jesus,* Hodder and Stoughton, 1986

Gardner, L., *Christianity Stands True,* College Press, 1994

Geisler, N. L., Nix, W., *A General Introduction to the Bible,* Moody Publishers, 1986

Green, J. et al., *Dictionary of Jesus and the Gospels,* InterVarsity, 1992

Greenlee, J. H., *Introduction to New Testament Textual Criticism*, Eerdmans, 1954

Groothuis, D. R., *Jesus in an Age of Controversy,* Harvest House, 1996

Gundry, R. H. , *Mark: A Commentary on his Apology for the Cross,* Eerdmans, 1993

Guthrie, D., *New Testament Introduction*, InterVarsity, 1990

Habermas, G., Licona, M., *The Case for the Resurrection of Jesus*, Kregel Publications, 2004

Habermas, G., *The Historical Jesus: Ancient Evidence for the Life of Christ,* College Press, 1996

Habermas, G., *The Resurrection Argument that Changed a Generation of Scholars,* Veritas Forum, http://www.veritas.org/resurrection-argument-changed-generation-scholars/, 2013

Hemer, C., *The Book of Acts in the Setting of Hellenistic History,* Eisenbrauns, 1990

Irenaeus, *Against Heresies*, 174 - 189 AD

J. Free, *Archaeology and Bible History*, Scripture Press, 1964

Jesus of Testimony, documentary film, https://www.youtube.com/watch?v=JAMODGaPRE8, accessed January, 6, 2020

Johnson, L., *The Real Jesus*, Harper San Francisco, 1996

Josephus, F., *Antiquities of the Jews,* Book 20, Chapter 9, 1, 93-94 AD

Kenyon, F., *The Bible and Archaeology*, Harper & Row, 1940

Lewis, C.S., *Mere Christianity*, Geoffrey Bles, 1952

Licona, M., *The Resurrection of Jesus: A New Historiographical Approach,* InterVarsity, 2010

Lumpkin, R., *The Physical Suffering of Christ*, J. Med. Assoc. Ala 47: 8-10, 1978.

Martyr, J., *Dialogue with Trypho,* 160 AD

Martyr, J., *First Apology*, 155 AD

Maslen, M.W., Mitchell, P. D., *Medical Theories on the Cause of Death in Crucifixion*, https://www.ncbi.nlm.nih.gov/pmc/articles/PMC1420788/, Journal of the Royal Society of Medicine, 99(4): 185–188, 2006

McDowell J., McDowell, S. *Evidence That Demands a Verdict: Life-Changing Truth for a Skeptical World,* Thomas Nelson, 2017

McDowell, J., *More than a Carpenter*, Tyndale Momentum, 1977

McDowell, S., *What is the Most Recent Manuscript Count for the New Testament?* https://seanmcdowell.org/blog/what-is-the-most-recent-manuscript-count-for-the-new-testament, accessed January, 5, 2020

McRay, J., *Archaeology and the New Testament,* Baker Academic, 2008

Meier, J., *A Marginal Jew: Rethinking the Historical Jesus,* Doubleday, 1991

Meier, J., *Marginal Jew,* Doubleday, 1991

Metherall, A., *Christ's Physical Suffering*, Firefighters for Christ, California

Miller, S., Huber, R., Hudson, L., *The Bible: A History: The Making and Impact of the Bible,* 2003

Neill, S., *The Interpretation of the New Testament*, Oxford University Press, 1964

NOAA, *The Significant Earthquake Database*, Year 33, Israel

Origen of Alexandria, *Against Celsus*, 248 AD

Phlegon of Tralles, *Olympiads*, 2nd century AD

Pitre, B., *The Case for Jesus,* Image Publishing, 2016

Pliny, *Letters*, http://faculty.georgetown.edu/jod/texts/pliny.html, accessed January, 5, 2020

Quake Reveals Day of Jesus' Crucifixion, Researchers Believe, NBC News, 2012, http://www.nbcnews.com/id/47555983/ns/technology_and_science-science/t/quake-reveals-day-jesus-crucifixion-researchers-believe/#.XhHJpJMzbOQ, accessed January, 6, 2020

Roberts, Donaldson, Coxe, *The Apology*, Volume 3, chapter 21, pp. 34–36, 1896

Robinson, J. A. T., *Redating the New Testament*, Wipf and Stock Publishers, 2000

Sanders, E.P., *The Historical Figure of Jesus*, Penguin, 1995

Sherwin-White, A. N., *Roman Society and Roman Law in the New Testament*, Wipf and Stock Publishers, 1963

Shrier, C., *The Science of the Crucifixion*, Azusa Pacific University, https://www.apu.edu/articles/15657/, accessed January, 6, 2020

Stanton, G., *The Gospels and Jesus*, 2nd. edition, Oxford University Press, 2002

Strobel, L., *The Case for Christ: A Journalist's Personal Investigation of the Evidence for Jesus*, Zondervan, 2016

Tabor, J., *Josephus' References to Crucifixion*, https://pages.uncc.edu/james-tabor/archaeology-and-the-dead-sea-scrolls/josephus-references-to-crucifixion/, accessed January, 5, 2020

Tacitus, *The Annals*, 1st century AD

Terasaka, D., *Medical Aspects of the Crucifixion of Jesus Christ*, https://www.blueletterbible.org/Comm/terasaka_david/misc/crucify.cfm, accessed January, 5, 2020

Tertullian, *Apologeticus*, 197 AD

The Letter of Pontius Pilate which He Wrote to the Roman Emperor concerning Our Lord Jesus Christ, taken from "The Early Church Fathers and Other Works" originally published by Wm. B. Eerdmans Pub. Co. in English in Edinburgh, Scotland, beginning in 1867. (ANF 8, Roberts and Donaldson). https://www.catholicculture.org/culture/library/fathers/view.cfm?recnum=1894, accessed January, 6, 2020

Wallace, D. B., Komoszewski, J. E., Sawyer, M. J., *Reinventing Jesus*, Kregel, 2006

Warfield, W., *The Person and Work of Christ*, Benediction Classics, 2015

Wilkins M., Moreland, J. P., *Jesus under Fire*, Zondervan, 1995

Williams, J. B., Schwab, M. J., Brauer, A., *An Early First-Century Earthquake in the Dead Sea*, International Geology Review, Volume 54, Issue 10, 2011

Wills, B., *Earthquakes in the Holy Land*, Geoscience World, Bulletin of Seismological Society of America, 1928

Chapter 2

Bethel TV, Testimonies, https://www.bethel.tv

Bird, C. E. et al., *Handbook of Medical Sociology,* Vanderbilt University Press, 2010

Bredesen, H., *Need a Miracle,* Praise Books, 1979

Brown, C.G., *Testing Prayer*, Harvard University Press, 2012

Brown, C.G. et al., *Study of the Therapeutic Effects of Proximal Intercessory Prayer (STEPP) on Auditory and Visual Impairments in Rural Mozambique*, Southern Medical Journal, Vol. 103, No. 9, 2010,

Brown, C.G., *Global Awakenings: Divine Healing Networks and Global Community in North America, Brazil, Mozambique and Beyond,* Oxford Scholarship Online, https://www.oxfordscholarship.com/view/10.1093/acprof:oso/9780195393408.001.0001/acprof-9780195393408-chapter-18, accessed January, 7, 2020

Brown, C.G., *Global Pentecostal and Charismatic Healing,* Oxford Scholarship Online, 2011

Brown, C.G., *Healing Words: Narratives of Spiritual Healing and Kathryn Kuhlman's Uses of Print Culture*, 1947-76, Religion and the Culture of Print in Modern America, 271-297, 2008.

Buckingham, J., *Daughter of Destiny: Kathryn Kuhlman*, Bridge-Logos Publishers, 1999

Casdorph, R., *The Miracles*, Bridge-Logos, 1976

CBN Miracle Testimonies, https://www1.cbn.com/700club/episodes/all/miracles, accessed January, 6, 2020. The website is constantly updated with new miracle testimonies.

Curlin, F. A. et al., *Religious Characteristics of U.S. Physicians: A National Survey,* Journal of General Internal Medicine 7:629-34, 2005, https://www.ncbi.nlm.nih.gov/pubmed/16050858, accessed January, 6, 2020

Danyun, *Lilies Amongst Thorns: Chinese Christians Tell Their Story through Blood and Tears,* 1991

DeGrandis, R., *Praying for Miracles*, 1990

Duffin, J., *Medical Miracles: Doctors, Saints and Healing in the Modern World,* Oxford University Press, 2009

Duvall, A., *Nothing But A Miracle Can Explain What Happened to this Texas Girl's Aggressive Brain Tumor,* December 20, 2018, https://hellochristian.com/11879-aggressive-inoperable-brain-tumor-threat-take-life-little-girl-texas-family-illness-prayer-miracle-medical-team-stun-roxli-doss-gofundme, accessed January, 6, 2020

Fahmy, D., *Key Findings about Americans' Belief in God,* April 25, 2018, https://www.pewresearch.org/fact-tank/2018/04/25/key-findings-about-americans-belief-in-god/, accessed January, 6, 2020

Faw, B., *Doctors, Patients, Prayer,* https://www.pbs.org/wnet/religionandethics/2009/10/23/october-23-2009-doctors-patients-and-prayer/4724/, October 23, 2009, accessed January, 6, 2020

Gardner, R., *Healing Miracles: A Doctor Investigates,* Darton, Longman and Todd, 1986

Godwin, B., *God's Strategy for Tragedy,* Deeper Revelation Books, 2008

Harper, E., The 700 Club, https://www.youtube.com/watch?v=iCIWVpxBwtE, accessed January, 6, 2020

Harris, R. W., *Acts Today: Signs and Wonders of the Holy Spirit,* Gospel Pub House 1998

Hulme, K., *Dial 'M' for Miracle,* https://www1.cbn.com/700club/dial-m-miracle, accessed January, 6, 2020

Keener, C., *Acts: An Exegetical Commentary Volume I: Introduction and 1:1-2:47,* Baker Academic, 2012

Keener, C., *Miracles: The Credibility of the New Testament Accounts,* Baker Academic, 2011

Kuhlman, K., *God Can Do It Again,* Prentice-Hall, 1969

Kuhlman, K., *I Believe in Miracles,* Bridge-Logos; Revised edition, 1992

Kuhlman, K., *Nothing is Impossible with God,* Bridge-Logos, 1974

Levine, J., *Doctors Explore Use of Prayer to Fight Disease,* CNN, July 13, 1996, quoted from *Miracle,* Keener, C.

Lewis, D. C., *Healing: Fiction, Fantasy or Fact?* Hodder & Stoughton Religious Division, 1989

MacMullen, R., *Christianizing the Roman Empire: A.D. 100-400,* Yale University Press, 1984

Manning, A., *Prayer Effective as Painkiller?*, USA Today, May 9, 2009, quoted from *Miracles*, Keener, C.

Miracle Woman, Time Magazine, September 14, 1970, http://content.time.com/time/magazine/article/0,9171,902774,00.html, accessed January, 6, 2020

Montgomery, D., *Faith Beyond Church Walls: Finding Freedom in Christ*, Compass Therapy, 2007

Moreland, J. P., *Kingdom Triangle: Recover the Christian Mind, Renovate the Soul, Restore the Spirit's Power*, Zondervan, 2017

Neil, E.G., *A Reporter Finds God Through Spiritual Healing*, Morehouse-Barlow, 1961

Nissen, H., *God of Miracles: A Danish Journalist Examines the Healings in the Ministry of Charles Ndifon*, Scandinavia, 2003

Orr, R. D., *Responding to Patient Beliefs in Miracles,* Southern Medical Journal, Volume 100, Number 12, 2007

Phillips, J., *Texas Girl's Inoperable Brain Tumor 'Miraculously' Disappears, Doctors Can't Explain Why,* August 29, 2019, https://www.theepochtimes.com/texas-girls-inoperable-brain-tumor-disappears-doctors-cant-explain-why_2741747.html, accessed January, 6, 2020

Polkinghorne, J., *Science and Providence*, 55, citing The Quarterly Review of the Churches' Fellowship for Physical and Spiritual Study, 125, 1985

Poll: Do You Believe In Miracles? CBN News, 1999, https://www.cbsnews.com/news/poll-do-you-believe-in-miracles/, accessed January, 6, 2020

Poloma, M., Green, J., *The Assemblies of God: Godly Love and the Revitalization of American Pentecostalism,* NYU Press, 2010

Prather, P., Prather, A., *We Believe in Miracles*, Impact Christian Books, 1995

Rauch, C., *Probing the Power of Prayer,* https://edition.cnn.com/2000/HEALTH/alternative/01/18/prayer.power.wmd/, 2000, accessed January, 6, 2020

Records of the Kathryn Kuhlman Foundation, https://www2.wheaton.edu/bgc/archives/guides/212.htm, accessed January, 6, 2020

Reed, W. S., *Surgery of the Soul*, Revell, 1969

Religion Among the Millennials, https://www.pewforum.org/2010/02/17/religion-among-the-millennials/, accessed January, 6, 2020

Remedios, D., https://www.youtube.com/watch?v=SoDyfdRaulw, accessed January, 6, 2020

Science or Miracles? Holiday Season Survey Reveals Physicians' Views on Faith, Prayer and Miracles, Business Wire, December 20, 2004, https://www.businesswire.com/news/home/20041220005244/en/Science-Miracle-Holiday-Season-Survey-Reveals-Physicians, accessed January, 6, 2020

Speed, T., *The Incurables: Unlock Healing for Spirit, Mind and Body*, Creation House, 2007

Spraggett, A., *Kathryn Kuhlman, The Woman Who Believes in Miracles*, Signet, 1971

Stewart, D., *Only Believe: Eye Witness Account of the Great Healing Revivals*, Destiny Image Publishers, 1999

Strobel, L., *The Case for Miracles: A Journalist Investigates Evidence for the Supernatural*, Zondervan, 2018

Studies Prove Healing Power of Prayer: More Doctors Praying with Patients, WESH, Orlando, 2004

Survey of Physicians' Views on Miracles, Louis Finkelstein Institute for Religious and Social Studies at the Louis Stein Center, 1999

van Natta, B., *A Miraculous Life: True Stories of Supernatural Encounters with God*, Charisma House, 2013

van Natta, B., https://sidroth.org/television/tv-archives/bruce-van-natta/, aired 19 January 2009, accessed January, 6, 2020

Warner, W., *Kathryn Kuhlman: The Woman Behind the Miracles*, Servant Pub., 1993

Wilson, M., *Miracle Reverses Damage to Heart Muscle*, https://www1.cbn.com/miracle-reverses-damage-heart-muscle, accessed January, 6, 2020

Winder, D., https://sidroth.org/television/tv-archives/delores-winder/, 2010, accessed January, 6, 2020

Winder, D., *Surprised by Healing: One of the Greatest Healing Miracles of the 21st Century*, Destiny Image Publishers, 2013

World Christian Doctors Network, http://www.wcdn.org/en/02_divinehealing/main.asp, accessed January, 6, 2020

Yeatts, C., *Power of Prayer, Kayla Knight on KLTV,* https://www.kltv.com/story/8699200/power-of-prayer-kayla-knight/, July 18, 2008, accessed January, 6, 2020

Young, E., *Survey: 9 in 10 Americans Believe in Miracles*, https://www.christianpost.com/news/survey-9-in-10-americans-believe-in-miracles.html, accessed January, 6, 2020

Chapter 3

Bonnke, R., *Raised from the Dead,* documentary film, 2001

Breakthrough, https://breakthroughmovie.com/truestory, accessed January, 6, 2020

Chavda, M., *Only Love Can Make a Miracle*, Mahesh Chavda Publisher, 2002

Crandall, C., *Raising the Dead: A Doctor Encounters the Miraculous*, FaithWords, 2012

George, S., *The Day God Raised Me from the Dead*, https://seangeorge.com.au/my-story/my-story/, accessed January, 6, 2020

Keener, C., *Miracles: The Credibility of the New Testament Accounts*, Raising the Dead, p. 536, Baker Academic, 2011. Several stories in this chapter are described in Keener's *Miracles*.

Missouri Boy Miraculously Recovers After Heart Stops While Submerged in Icy Water, February 9, 2015, https://www.nydailynews.com/life-style/health/boy-survives-icy-water-15-minutes-article-1.2108787, accessed January, 6, 2020

Missouri Teens Miracle Recovery, February 10, 2015, https://www.today.com/news/missouri-teens-miracle-recovery-after-underwater-15-minutes-t1381, accessed January, 6, 2020

Mom Prays, Dead Son Comes Back to Life, USA Today, February 5, 2015, https://www.usatoday.com/videos/news/nation-now/2015/02/05/22895679/, accessed January, 6, 2020

Piper, D., Murphey, C., *90 Minutes in Heaven: A True Story of Death and Life,* Revell, 2014

Chapter 4

Abanes, R., *Harry Potter and the Bible: The Menace Behind the Magick*, Horizon Books, 2001

Aird, R. L., et. al., *Is the New Age Phenomenon Connected to Delusion-like Experiences? Analysis of Survey Data from Australia,* Mental Health Religion & Culture, 13(1), 2010

Aird, R. L., et. al., *Religion, Spirituality, and Mental Health and Social Behaviour in Young Adulthood: A Longitudinal Study,* 2009

Albanese, M. J., *Demons & Possession, New Oxford Review,* June 2008, https://www.newoxfordreview.org/documents/letter-to-the-editor-june-2008/, accessed January, 7, 2020

Bailey, A., *The Rays and the Initiations,* Vol. V, *A Treatise on the Seven Rays*, Lucis Publishing Co., 1960

Betty, S., *The Growing Evidence for 'Demonic Possession:' What Should Psychiatry's Response Be?,* Journal of Religion and Health, Vol. 44, No. 1, pp. 13-30, 2005, https://www.jstor.org/stable/27512832, accessed January, 7, 2020

Blavatsky, H.P., *The Secret Doctrine,* Vol III, 1888, Theosophical University Press, 1970 ("Verbatim with the original edition, 1888")

Blavatsky, H.P., *The Secret Doctrine: The Synthesis of Science, Religion, and Philosophy*, Vol. I - Cosmogenesis, Theosophical University Press, 1970 ("Verbatim with the original edition, 1888")

Blavatsky, H.P., *The Secret Doctrine: The Synthesis of Science, Religion, and Philosophy*, Vol. II - Anthropogenesis, Theosophical University Press, 1970 ("Verbatim with the original edition, 1888")

Brooks, A., *Witchcraft Goes Mainstream*, Harvest House, 2004

Buddhist Deities, https://en.wikipedia.org/wiki/Buddhist_deities, accessed January 9, 2020

Buddhist Deities, Fierce, https://en.wikipedia.org/wiki/Fierce_deities, accessed January 9, 2020

Could Neo-paganism be the New 'Religion' of America?, Big Think, September 30, 2019, https://bigthink.com/culture-religion/modern-paganism, accessed January, 7, 2020

Cyr, R., *Modern Wicca and the Witchcraft Movement*, NEXT: Vol. 6, article 2. https://scholar.colorado.edu/next/vol6/iss1/2, 2019, accessed January, 7, 2020

Demand for Exorcisms Growing with Decline of Christianity, Priests Say, The Christian Post, April 17, 2018, https://www.christianpost.com/news/demand-for-exorcisms-growing-with-decline-of-christianity-priests-say.html, accessed January, 7, 2020

Demonic Possession is Real and Victims Seeking Exorcism Should Not be Ignored': Prominent Psychiatrist on the World Beyond, The Telegraph UK, June 3, 2018, https://www.telegraph.co.uk/news/2018/06/03/demonic-possession-real-victims-seeking-exorcism-should-not/, accessed January, 7, 2020

Demonic Possession is Real, Says Psychiatry Professor Who's Spent 25 Years Viewing Exorcisms, Daily Mail Australia, June 20, 2018, https://www.dailymail.co.uk/news/article-5857677/Psychiatrist-professor-says-demonic-possession-real-witnessing-exorcisms-25-years.html, accessed January, 7, 2020

DIY Religions More Harm than Good, Brisbane Times, January 18, 2008, https://www.brisbanetimes.com.au/national/queensland/diy-religions-more-harm-than-good-20080118-ge9kft.html, accessed January, 7, 2020

Exorcisms Booming as Christian Faith Declines and Internet Offers Easy Access to Black Magic, Priests Told, April 16, 2018, https://www.telegraph.co.uk/news/2018/04/16/casting-demons-catholic-priests-perform-exorcisms-phone-demand/, accessed January, 7, 2020

Exorcist Explains Why Demand for Exorcisms Has Risen, WKRC, September 28, 2019, https://kutv.com/news/nation-world/interview-with-an-exorcist, accessed January, 7, 2020

Farias, M. et al., *Personality and Cognitive Predictors of New Age Practices and Beliefs,* Personality and Individual Differences, 39(5), 979-989, 2005

Gadit, A. M., *Demonic-Possession Phenomenon Merits Scientific Study,* Psychiatric News, American Psychiatric Association, March 16, 2007, https://psychnews.psychiatryonline.org/doi/full/10.1176/pn.42.6.0012a, accessed January, 7, 2020

Gallagher, R., *As a Psychiatrist I Diagnose Mental Illness. Also, I Help Spot with Demonic Possession. How a Scientist Learned to Work with Exorcist,* Washington Post, July 1, 2016, https://www.washingtonpost.com/posteverything/wp/2016/07/01/as-a-psychiatrist-i-diagnose-mental-illness-and-sometimes-demonic-possession/, accessed January, 7, 2020

Gallagher, R., *Demonic Foes: My Twenty-Five Years as a Psychiatrist Investigating Possessions, Diabolic Attacks and the Paranormal,* HarperCollins, 2020

Hindu Deities, https://en.wikipedia.org/wiki/Hindu_deities, accessed January 9, 2020

Hubbard, B.M., *The Revelation: A Message of Hope for the New Millennium*, Nataraj Publishing, 1995

Innocent, M., *Potter's Field: Harry Potter and the Popularization of Witchcraft*, The Orthodox Word, no. 220, pp. 241-55, 2001

Jacobs, C., *Deliver Us From Evil*, Chosen Books, 2001

Johnson, W. C., *Demon Possession and Mental Illness*, JASA 34: 149-154, 1982, https://www.asa3.org/ASA/PSCF/1982/JASA9-82Johnson.html, accessed January, 7, 2020

Keener, C., *Miracles: The Credibility of the New Testament Accounts, Appendix B, Spirit Possession and Exorcism in Societies Today*, p. 837, Baker Academic, 2011

King, M., et al., *Religion, Spirituality and Mental Health: Results from a National Study of English Households,* The British Journal of Psychiatry, Volume 202, Issue 1, pp. 68-73, 2013, https://www.cambridge.org/core/journals/the-british-journal-of-psychiatry/article/religion-spirituality-and-mental-health-results-from-a-national-study-of-english-households/434CFF0E75402B578ED0149600BF55A4#BIBL, accessed January, 7, 2020

King, M., *Religion, Mental Health and Ethnicity. EMPIRIC – A National Survey of England*, Journal of Mental Health, 15(2), 153-162, 2006, https://www.tandfonline.com/doi/abs/10.1080/09638230600608891, accessed January, 7, 2020

Koch, K. E., *Christian Counseling and Occultism: A Complete Guidebook to Occult Oppression and Deliverance,* Kregel Publications, 1972

Koch, K. E., *Occult ABC: Exposing Occult Practices and Ideologies*, Kregel Publications, 1978

Koch, K. E., *Occult Bondage and Deliverance: Counseling the Occultly Oppressed,* Kregel Publications, 1972

Koenig, H. G., *Concerns About Measuring "Spirituality" in Research,* The Journal of Nervous and Mental Disease, 196(5), 349-355 310.1097/NMD, 2008

Lewandowski, K. E., et al., *Anxiety and Depression Symptoms in Psychometrically Identified Schizotypy*, Schizophrenia Research, 83(2–3), 225-235, 2006, https://www.sciencedirect.com/science/article/abs/pii/S0920996405013903?via%3Dihub, accessed January, 7, 2020

Lindeman, M., Aarnio, K., *Superstitious, Magical and Paranormal Beliefs: An Integrative Model,* Journal of Research in Personality, 41(4), 731-744, 2007

Lipka, M., Gecewicz, C., *More Americans Now Say They're Spiritual but Not Religious,* September 6, 2017, https://www.pewresearch.org/fact-tank/2017/09/06/more-americans-now-say-theyre-spiritual-but-not-religious/, accessed January, 7, 2020

MacNutt, F., *Deliverance from Evil Spirits,* Chosen Books, 1995

Malia, L., *A Fresh Look at a Remarkable Document: Exorcism: The Report of a Commission Convened by the Bishop of Exeter,* Anglican Theological Review, 83(1), 65–88, 2001

Martin, M., *Hostage to the Devil: The Possession and Exorcism of Five Americans,* HarperOne, 2013

Mercado, M. C., et al., *Trends in Emergency Department Visits for Nonfatal Self-inflicted Injuries Among Youth Aged 10 to 24 Years in the United States,* 2001-2015, JAMA. 318(19): 1931-1933, 2017, https://jamanetwork.com/journals/jama/fullarticle/2664031, accessed January, 7, 2020

Miller, D. E., Yamamori, T., *Global Pentecostalism: The New Face of Christian Social Engagement,* University of California Press, 2007

More Kids Are Attempting and Thinking About Suicide, According to a New Study, Time Magazine, May 16, 2018, http://time.com/5279029/suicide-rates-rising-study/, accessed January, 7, 2020

Mullen, G., *There's a Battle for Your Mind,* June 1, 2011, https://drgrantmullen.com/uncategorized/theres-a-battle-for-your-mind/, accessed January, 7, 2020

New Religious Beliefs Focus Too Much on Self, The University of Queensland Press Release, January 17, 2008, https://www.uq.edu.au/news/article/2008/01/new-religious-beliefs-focus-too-much-self,, accessed 7 January 2018

Occult Sites 'Lure' Teenagers, BBC News, April 22, 2000, http://news.bbc.co.uk/2/hi/in_depth/education/2000/unions_2000/722283.stm, accessed January, 7, 2020

Oregon-based Exorcist Says Demonic Possession Cases Are Getting Darker, The Christian Post, September 30, 2019, https://www.christianpost.com/news/oregon-based-exorcist-says-demonic-possession-cases-are-getting-darker.html, accessed January, 7, 2020

Peck, J. et al., *The Second Coming of the New Age,* Defender Publishing, 2018

Peck, M. S., *Glimpses of the Devil: A Psychiatrist's Personal Accounts of Possession,* Free Press, 2009

Peck, M. S., *People of the Lie*, New York: Simon and Schuster, 1983

Psychiatrists Can't Explain Demonic Possession, Says Director of The Exorcist, November 2, 2016, https://catholicherald.co.uk/news/2016/11/02/psychiatrists-cant-explain-demonic-possession-says-director-of-the-exorcist/, accessed January, 7, 2020

Rose, S., *Orthodoxy and the Religion of the Future,* St. Herman Press, 1992

Saucier, G., Skrzypińska, K., *Spiritual But Not Religious? Evidence for Two Independent Dispositions. Journal of Personality,* 74(5), 1257-1292, 2006

Spangler, D., *Reflections on the Christ,* Findhorn Lecture Series, 3rd edition, 1981

'Spiritual' People at Higher Risk of Mental Health Problems, The Telegraph UK, January 2, 2013, https://www.telegraph.co.uk/news/health/news/9774259/Spiritual-people-at-higher-risk-of-mental-health-problems.html, accessed January, 7, 2020

Suicide Rate Rises Among Young People in England and Wales. Rate among Girls Aged 15-19 Hits Record High; Rate Among Men of All Ages in UK is Falling. https://www.theguardian.com/society/2018/sep/04/suicide-rate-rises-among-young-people-in-england-and-wales, accessed January, 7, 2020

Suicide Rates Rising Across the U.S., June 7, 2018, https://www.cdc.gov/media/releases/2018/p0607-suicide-prevention.html, accessed January, 7, 2020

Sumrall, L., *Bitten by Devils: The Supernatural Account of a Young Girl Bitten by Unseen Demons, Documented by Medical Doctors and Her Miraculous Deliverance that Would Bring Revival to a Nation,* LeSEA Publishing Co., South Bend, Indiana, USA, 1987, https://drlestersumrall.com/books/bitten-by-devils/, accessed January, 7, 2020

Teen Suicide is Soaring, USA Today, March 19, 2018, https://www.usatoday.com/story/news/politics/2018/03/19/teen-suicide-soaring-do-spotty-mental-health-and-addiction-treatment-share-blame/428148002/, accessed January, 7, 2020

Teenage Suicides in England and Wales Rise 67% Since 2010, The Independent, September 4, 2018, https://www.independent.co.uk/news/uk/home-news/teenage-suicides-england-and-wales-2010-ons-a8522331.html, accessed January, 7, 2020

The Global Religious Landscape, A Report on the Size and Distribution of the World's Major Religious Groups as of 2010, Pew Templeton Global Religious Futures Project, 2012, https://assets.pewresearch.org/wp-content/uploads/sites/11/2014/01/global-religion-full.pdf, accessed January, 7, 2020

The U.S. Suicide Rate Has Increased 30% since 2000, and Tripled for Young Girls, Business Insider Australia, June 14, 2018, https://www.businessinsider.com.au/us-suicide-rate-increased-since-2000-2018-6?r=US&IR=T, accessed January, 7, 2020

The U.S. Witch Population Has Seen an Astronomical Rise, Quartz, October 5, 2018, https://qz.com/quartzy/1411909/the-explosive-growth-of-witches-wiccans-and-pagans-in-the-us/, accessed January, 7, 2020

U.S. Suicide Rate Surges to a 30-year High, The New York Times, April 22, 2016, https://www.nytimes.com/2016/04/22/health/us-suicide-rate-surges-to-a-30-year-high.html, accessed January, 7, 2020

U.S. Suicide Rate Surges to Three Decade High, April 22, 2016, https://www.chicagotribune.com/nation-world/ct-us-suicide-rate-20160422-story.html, accessed January, 7, 2020

van Gelder D. W., *A Case of Demon Possession,* Journal of Pastoral Care & Counseling, 41(2), 151–161, 1987, https://journals.sagepub.com/doi/10.1177/002234098704100208, accessed January, 7, 2020

Vernon, M., *Spiritual, but Not Religious? A Dangerous Mix,* https://www.theguardian.com/commentisfree/belief/2013/jan/09/spiritual-but-not-religious-dangerous-mix, accessed January, 7, 2020

What's behind the rise in youth suicides?, CBS News, November 21, 2017, https://www.cbsnews.com/news/suicide-youth-teens-whats-behind-rise/, accessed January, 7, 2020

When Exorcists Need Help, They Call Him, CNN, August 4, 2017, https://edition.cnn.com/2017/08/04/health/exorcism-doctor/index.html, accessed January, 7, 2020

Wicca, Wikipedia article and list of references, https://en.wikipedia.org/wiki/Horned_God, accessed January, 7, 2020

Wilson, W. P., *Demon Possession and Exorcism,* Journal of Psychology and Theology, Vol. 17, No. 2, 135-139, 1989, https://journals.sagepub.com/doi/pdf/10.1177/009164718901700206, accessed January, 7, 2020

Wilson, W. P., *Manuscript on Demonization & Deliverance,* http://www.blendedbody.com/_cl/_audio/_2ndgen/CenturyOfSelf/MiscDocuments/Warnings/PDF%20Demonization%20and%20Deliverance.pdf, accessed January, 7, 2020

Witch Population Doubles as Millennials Cast off Christianity, New York Post, November 20, 2018, https://nypost.com/2018/11/20/witch-population-doubles-as-millennials-cast-off-christianity/, accessed January, 7, 2020

Youth Suicidal Behavior is on the Rise, Especially Among Girls, The Wall Street Journal, May 15, 2018, https://www.wsj.com/articles/youth-suicidal-behavior-is-on-the-rise-especially-among-girls-1526443782, accessed January, 7, 2020

Chapter 5

Bellg, L., *Near-Death in the ICU*, Sloan Press, 2015

Bonenfant, R. J., *A Child's Encounter with the Devil: An Unusual Near-Death Experience with Both Blissful and Frightening Elements*, Journal of Near-Death Studies 20(2), pp. 87-100, 2001

Burke, J., *Imagine Heaven: Near-Death Experiences, God's Promises, and the Exhilarating Future that Awaits You*, Baker Books, 2015

Burpo, T., *Heaven is for Real*, Thomas Nelson, 2010

Bush, N. E., Greyson, B., *Distressing Near-Death Experiences: The Basics*, Mo Med.T,111(6): 486 - 491, 2014

Bush, N. E., *Afterward: Making Meaning After a Frightening Near-Death Experience*, Journal of Near-Death Studies 21(2), pp. 99-133, 2002

Bush, N. E., *Dancing Past the Dark: Distressing Near-death Experiences*, 2012

Crandall, C. *Touching Heaven: A Cardiologist's Encounters with Death and Living Proof of an Afterlife*, FaithWords, 2016

Crandall, C., CBN, https://www1.cbn.com/video/looking-beyond-the-limitations-of-science?show=700club, accessed January, 6, 2020

Dale, L., *From Fear to Love,* Journal of Near-Death Studies, 25(3), 171-179, 2007

Distressing Near-Death-Experiences, https://iands.org/distressing-near-death-experiences.html, accessed January, 7, 2020

Ellwood, G. F., *The Uttermost Deep: The Challenge of Near-Death Experiences*, Lantern, 2001

Gallup, G. Jr., Proctor, W., *Adventures in Immortality: A Look Beyond The Threshold of Death*, McGraw Hill, 1982

Greyson, B., Bush, N.E., *Distressing Near-Death Experiences,* Bailey, L. W., Yates, J. (Eds.), *The Near-Death Experience: A Reader,* Routledge, 1996

Greyson, B., *Incidence and Correlates of Near-Death Experiences on a Cardiac Care Unit,* General Hospital Psychiatry, 25, 269-276, 2003

Greyson, B., *Near-Death Experiences in a Psychiatric Outpatient Clinic Population*, Psychiatric Services, December, Vol. 54, No. 12. The American Psychiatric Association, 2003

Greyson, B., *Near-Death Experiences,* In E. Cardea, Lynn, S. J. and Krippner S. (Eds.), Varieties of Anomalous Experiences, American Psychological Association, 315-352, 2000

Habermas, G., Moreland, J.P., *Beyond Death: Explore the Evidence for Immortality*, Wipf & Stock Pub, 2004

Hagan, J.C. III, Van Way, C. W., *The Science of Near-Death Experiences*, University of Missouri Press, 2018

Holden, J. M., Greyson, B., James, D., *The Handbook of Near-Death Experience: Thirty Years of Investigation*, Praeger, 2009

I Saw Jesus in Heaven and He Knew My Name, Says Doctor Who Had Near-Death Experience, Christian Today, August 14, 2016, https://www.christiantoday.com/article/i-saw-jesus-in-heaven-and-he-knew-my-name-says-doctor-who-had-near-death-experience/93076.htm, accessed January, 7, 2020

International Association for Near-Death Studies, database, https://iands.org/component/finder/search.html?q=jesus&Itemid=254, accessed January, 7, 2020

Jesus Christ and the Near-Death Experience, database, https://www.near-death.com/science/research/jesus.html, accessed January, 7, 2020

Landon, *Dead Boy Returns From Afterlife to Tell His Mom About Heaven*, https://www.youtube.com/watch?v=4eTKh7xM7DQ&t=277s, accessed January 9, 2020

Lewis, C.S. *On the Logic of Drawing History from Ancient Documents, Especially from Testimonies*, published 1958 in Collected Papers of Charles Sanders Peirce, 1901, retrieved from http://www.iupui.edu/~peirce/

Long, J., *God and the Afterlife*, Harper Collins, 2016

Long, J., Perry, P., *Evidence of the Afterlife: The Science of Near-Death Experiences*, HarperOne, 2010

M., Perry, P., *Closer to the Light: Learning from the Near-death Experiences of Children,* Villard, 1990

Moody, R., *Life After Life,* Bantam, 1979

Moody, R., *The Light Beyond,* Bantam, 1989

Near Death Experiences with Gary Habermas, December 7, 2018, https://www.biola.edu/blogs/think-biblically/2018/near-death-experiences, accessed January, 7, 2020

Near-Death Experience Research Foundation, database, https://nderf.org

Nelson, L., *Beyond the Veil*, Cedar Fort, 1988

Price, J.W., *Revealing Heaven: The Christian Case for Near-Death Experiences,* HarperOne, 2013

Rawlings, M., *Beyond Death's Door*, Bantam, 1991

Rawlings, M., *To Hell and Back*, Thomas Nelson, 1993

Ritchie, G., *Return to Tomorrow*, Baker Publishing Group, 1995

Rommer, B., *Blessing in Disguise: Another Side of the Near Death Experience*, Llewellyn Publications, 2000

Sabom, M. B., *The Near-Death Experience: Myth or Reality? A Methodological Approach*, https://digital.library.unt.edu/ark:/67531/metadc1052005/m2/1/high_res_d/vol1-no1-44.pdf, accessed January, 7, 2020

Sabom, M., *Light and Death*, Zondervan, 1998

Sam Parnia et al., *AWARE—AWAreness during REsuscitation—A Prospective Study*, Volume 85, Issue 12, Pages 1799–1805, 2014, https://www.resuscitationjournal.com/article/S0300-9572%2814%2900739-4/fulltext, accessed January, 7, 2020

Sartori, P. *Wisdom of Near-Death Experiences*, Watkins Publishing, 2014

Sleutjes, A. et al., *Almost 40 Years Investigating Near-Death Experiences: An Overview of Mainstream Scientific Journals*, The Journal of Nervous and Mental Disease 202 11: 833-6, 2014

Storm, H., *My Descent Into Death: A Second Chance at Life*, Harmony, 2005

The Near-Death of a Child, http://nhne-pulse.org/the-near-death-of-a-child/, accessed January, 7, 2020

van Lommel, P. et al., *Near-death Experience in Survivors of Cardiac Arrest: A Prospective Study*, Lancet, 358, 2039-2045, 2001

van Lommel, P., *Consciousness Beyond Life: The Science of the Near-death Experience*, HarperOne, 2010

van Lommel, P., *Getting Comfortable With Near-Death Experiences: Dutch Prospective Research on Near-Death Experiences During Cardiac Arrest*, Mo. Med., 111(2): 126–131, 2014

Chapter 6

Afshin, J., https://www.youtube.com/watch?v=kcXGQX-LPPM, accessed January, 7, 2020

Ali, https://www.youtube.com/watch?v=LAJepZ1Nm94, accessed January, 7, 2020

Beardsworth, T., *A Sense of Presence: The Phenomenology of Certain Kinds of Visionary and Ecstatic Experience based on a Thousand Contemporary First-hand Accounts*, Oxford: Religious Experience Research Unit, Manchester College, 1977

Brewer, E.C., *A Dictionary of Miracles*, Chatto & Windus, 1884

Casdorph, R., *The Miracles*, Bridge-Logos, 1976, accessed January, 7, 2020

Christian, Jr., W. A., *Apparitions in Late Medieval and Renaissance Spain,* Princeton University Press, 1981

Cody, C. A. J., *Testimony: A Philosophical Study,* Clarendon Press, 1992

DuPre, C., https://sidroth.org/television/tv-archives/chris-dupre/, accessed January, 7, 2020

Flashman, R., https://www.oneforisrael.org/bible-based-teaching-from-israel/video/jewish-testimonies-i-met-messiah/dr-rich-flashman-how-i-met-messiah/, accessed January, 7, 2020

Ghazal, A., https://www1.cbn.com/700club/amy-ghazal-dreaming-jesus, accessed January, 7, 2020

Gibson, J., *The Senses Considered as Perceptual Systems,* Greenwood Press, 1966

Habermas, G., *The Case for the Resurrection of Jesus,* Kregel Publications, 2004

Hollands, E., https://www.youtube.com/watch?v=HxD15fSgsRg, accessed January, 7, 2020

Ilibagiza, I., *The Boy Who Met Jesus,* Hay House, 2012

James, J., *Essays in Psychical Research,* Harvard University Press, https://www.hup.harvard.edu/catalog.php?isbn=9780674267084, accessed January, 7, 2020

Jesus of Testimony, documentary film, https://www.youtube.com/watch?v=JAMODGaPRE8, accessed January, 6, 2020

Miller, T. A., *Did Jesus Really Rise from the Dead? A Surgeon-Scientist Examines the Evidence,* Crossway, 2013

More than Dreams, morethandreams.org. Tells the compelling, true stories of five Muslims from five countries who share one life-changing experience. Each of them saw Jesus Christ in a dream or a vision and their lives were forever transformed.

Ndifon, C., https://www.youtube.com/watch?v=qWgetTfrK38, accessed January, 7, 2020

Osborn, T.L., *Jesus Visited Hour House,* https://osborn.org, accessed January, 7, 2020

Perez, A., https://www.youtube.com/watch?v=ys_eR6i4fGM, accessed January, 7, 2020

Perior, P. https://www.youtube.com/watch?v=dtt6BGQvgdQ, accessed January, 7, 2020

Perry, D., https://www.youtube.com/watch?v=TyAlk198oxE, accessed January, 7, 2020

Pitre, B., *The Case for Jesus,* Image Publishing, 2016

Siddiki, N., https://www.youtube.com/watch?v=52UChmWddW8, accessed January, 7, 2020

Singh, S., https://www.christianity.com/church/church-history/timeline/1901-2000/sundar-singhs-vision-of-christ-11630674.html, accessed January, 7, 2020

Suleiman, S., https://www.youtube.com/watch?v=HR1E1ZWgb4o, accessed January, 7, 2020

Tanis, D., https://www.youtube.com/watch?v=F2UpLmEjV5U, accessed January, 7, 2020

Tour, J., https://www.youtube.com/watch?v=QNGLZvtRoiU&feature=emb_logo, accessed 7, January 2020

Wallace, J. W., *Cold-Case Christianity: A Homicide Detective Investigates the Claims of the Gospels,* David C. Cook, 2013

Walsh, W. J., *The Apparitions and Shrines of Heaven's Bright Queen*, Forgotten Books, 2018

Wiebe, P. H., *Visions of Jesus*, Oxford University Press, 1997

Zaucha, R., http://www1.cbn.com/700club/ron-zaucha-vision-jesus, accessed January, 7, 2020

Chapter 7

C. W., Welty, W. P., *I, Jesus. An Autobiography*, Missler, Koinonia Institute, 2014

Made in the USA
Middletown, DE
02 March 2020